DEATH *at the* CECIL HOTEL *in* LOS ANGELES

DALE RICHARD PERELMAN

THE
History
PRESS

Published by The History Press
Charleston, SC
www.historypress.com

First published 2022

Manufactured in the United States

ISBN 9781467150187

Library of Congress Control Number: 2022931451

Notice: The information in this book is true and complete to the best of our knowledge. It is offered without guarantee on the part of the author or The History Press. The author and The History Press disclaim all liability in connection with the use of this book.

CONTENTS

The Cecil Hotel sign, 2021. *Courtesy of Sean Kanan.*

ACKNOWLEDGEMENTS

T hanks to my wonderful wife, supporter and reader, Michele; my writer son, Sean Kanan, who provided me with the idea for this book; and my daughter, Robyn Bernstein, for being my daughter and a great writer as well.

This is my fourth book with The History Press, and my acquisitions editor, Banks Smither, has again provided his invaluable support. I also appreciate the hard work and support of my editor Ashley Hill.

The author in front of the Cecil Hotel. *Author's collection.*

INTRODUCTION

Her body struck the canopy of the Cecil Hotel with a thud. Another victim had died. One witness released a high-pitched scream. The horrific spectacle unhinged a frail-looking man, who sobbed and mumbled incoherently at the sight, his arms flailing while he turned and fled toward the Philharmonic Hall.

Within minutes, the wail of a siren from an oncoming police cruiser filled the air, interrupting the growing crowd's gasps and groans. A fire department emergency vehicle hastened to the front of the hotel to remove the woman's body—another death at the Cecil.

Guests labeled the Cecil "Hotel Suicide." The media and paranormalists designated it as the most haunted hotel in Los Angeles. All three groups were right. Inexplicable fatalities, suicides, drug overdoses, murders and violence had snowballed throughout the years. A mishmash of misfits snaked through the Cecil Hotel's doors, enticed by its cheap rates and convenient downtown location, only to succumb to despair and sometimes death.

Like a black widow spider luring an unsuspecting fly into its web, the hotel drew the impoverished, the mentally ill, the lost and the drug-addicted to its rooms. The sketchy area around Skid Row wallowed in sex offenders, cutthroats, killers, thieves and drug dealers, many of whom feasted on the Hotel Cecil's lax security. Some acted as predators; others became prey.

Reputation remains a fragile commodity. It can change like a chameleon in a matter of seconds or ooze into oblivion like molasses. A single mishap can rupture a person or place. Joe Paterno, the once highly regarded Penn State

An interior view looking into the lobby of the Cecil Hotel. *Image from the Historical-Cultural Monument application, City of Los Angeles.*

football coach, plummeted from grace, either justly or unjustly, depending on whom you ask, once the Jerry Sandusky child molestation incident came to light. In the case of the Cecil, the decline came gradually.

The hotel opened with fanfare and a five-star rating in 1924. Its prestige remained near the top for several years—that is, until the Great Depression and a cascade of unfortunate occurrences dragged it into an abyss. Now home to ghosts of the past, surrounded by a once-booming financial district, a lively transportation system and a vibrant retail scene, the nearly empty Cecil Hotel sits like poet Percy Bysshe Shelley's solitary statue of Ozymandias, set in a desert of dilapidated buildings on the edge of Skid Row.

> *Look on my works ye mighty and despair!*
> *Nothing beside remains. Round the decay*
> *of that colossal wreck, boundless and bare*
> *the lone and level sands stretch far away.*

The young man stepped off the curb without looking, his thoughts floating elsewhere. A speeding car struck and killed him. He awakened standing by Heaven's pearly gates, with Saint Peter sitting at a desk in front of him.

"Well, son, I've checked, and you are free to make a choice between Heaven and Hell. Would you like to take a look at both options?"

"Yes, sir."

In the blink of an eye, the newly arrived decedent floated atop a cloud in the sky. A cherub sat beside him, strumming a lyre. A handful of angels watched silently and blissfully while savoring the soft, melodious music.

"How beautiful," said the man to Saint Peter. "But I guess I should visit Hell as well."

"And so you shall."

With a snap of Saint Peter's fingers, the man found himself in Hell. Sexy beauties in scanty outfits swayed to the smooth sounds of jazz. The intoxicating perfume from the dancers wafted across the room. A smiling bartender poured margaritas for the patrons. A cornucopia of delectable canapés covered a long table. Heaven appeared sweet and serene, but Hell rocked.

"Well, how do you choose?" asked Saint Peter. "But I must caution you—whichever one you pick, you can never change your mind. Your decision is irreversible. Do you understand?"

"I do," the recruit said. "Heaven looked great, but Hell looked like lots more fun. I choose Hell."

"And so you shall have it," said Saint Peter.

A sketch of Satan. *Image from Creative Commons.*

The man quickly found himself in the fires of Hell. The food and drinks had disappeared. The women he had seen dancing appeared old and haggard. Heavy chains held them in place. When he looked at his own wrists and ankles, manacles blocked his movement. Fierce guard dogs snarled and snapped at his feet.

The unfortunate man looked up to see Satan towering over him.

"This is not what I thought I was getting. What happened to the food, the dancing girls, the wine and the music?"

"Ah," said Satan with a grin. "Appearances can be deceiving. What you first saw was for prospects, but now that you have entered my domain as a full-time resident, things are quite different." Satan roared with laughter.

Like Satan's false presentation of the joys of Hell, the magnificent entryway and classic lobby of the Cecil Hotel beckoned visitors through its doors, masking a scary and dangerous place. What appeared at first like a virtual paradise in the heart of downtown Los Angeles proved to be a mirage. Rather than a guarantee of peace and safety, guests found themselves in a crypt of horrors—trapped like the poor soul in the story.

1

THE ROARING TWENTIES

The story of the Cecil began on Saturday, December 20, 1924, with the formal opening of the hotel. Los Angeles's economy boomed during the Roaring Twenties. With Christmas less than a week away, throngs of shoppers filled the downtown streets. The clink of coins echoed from the pockets of the populace. Optimism ruled the day.

During the past decade, the city's population had doubled to more than one million inhabitants, making it the country's fifth-largest city behind New York, Chicago, Philadelphia and Detroit. Center city Los Angeles emerged as the financial, commercial and entertainment hub of the West Coast. Nearly half the city lived and worked in the downtown area.

In 1924, Eddie Cantor's "Doodle-Doo-Doo" topped the popular music charts. Bandleader Paul Specht's Hotel Orchestra's rendition of "Baghdad" landed solidly at the number two spot. Arthur Gibbs and his Gang's "The Charleston" followed close behind the leaders.

Frank Lloyd Productions Incorporated's swashbuckling silent movie *The Sea Hawk* headed up the nation's box office receipts with a tally of $2.00 million. The comedy *Girl Shy*, starring Harold Lloyd, came in a distant second with receipts of $1.55 million.

Although radio remained in its infancy, Los Angeles station KFSG featured evangelist Sister Aimee Semple McPherson's popular and inspirational *Sunshine Show* at 7:00 a.m.

Calvin Coolidge held the presidency of the staunchly Republican country, and George E. Cryer reigned as a three-term mayor of Los Angeles. Earlier in the year, the Municipal Art Commission approved architect Bertram Goodhue's design for an ultramodern, state-of-the-art library on West Fifth Street. City council bandied about various renditions for a new city hall building, pegged for completion within the next few years.

In the United States, the average annual income was about $2,196.00 (approximately $33,510.00 today). The *Los Angeles Times* cost $0.09, a loaf of bread cost $0.09, the cost to mail a letter was $0.02 and a postcard cost just $0.01. Downtown dentist Dr. Fairfield charged $1.00 for a filling, and Dr. Carr installed a twenty-two-carat-gold crown for $5.00. Platt Music advertised an upright piano for $194.00, and a new Ford automobile cost its owner just $360.00.

As the center city hustled and bustled with activity, cars, trolleys, buses and taxi cabs jammed the streets. Pedestrian walkways hummed with purpose. Cranes, piles of bricks, concrete blocks, steel beams, spools of electrical wire and sundry materials for upcoming construction projects compounded the congestion.

Downtown churches and religious structures projected an aura of grandeur and spirituality. First Baptist, Epiphany Lutheran, First United Presbyterian, Broadway Christian, Christadelphian Ecclesia, First Friends, the B'nai Brith Synagogue and La Iglesia de Nuestra Señora la Reina de Los Ángeles stood out among the numerous religious congregations dotting the landscape. A heavy concentration of white, Anglo-Saxon Protestants, primarily Methodists, composed the bulk of the area's population. However, an influx of minorities—Latinos, Black people, Asians and other immigrants—had recently altered the area's demographics.

The center city functioned as Los Angeles's core shopping district. The area featured scores of retail purveyors specializing in millinery, lingerie, clothing, jewelry, electronics, housewares, books and toys. Barbershops, beauty parlors, laundry facilities, apothecaries and physicians served the physical needs of the locals. Police and firefighters protected both businesses and citizens alike. Schools, a hospital, parks, new roads, sewers, waterworks and public transportation mushroomed the downtown area's infrastructure.

With Christmas only five days away, jewelry advertisements filled the *Los Angeles Times*. Geo. D. Davidson on South Spring Street promoted a fourteen-karat gold Waltham pocket watch for $40.00. Montgomery Brothers, the city's oldest jeweler, advertised French-made La Tausca princess- and matinee-length pearl strands for $10.00. Slavicks plugged a $50.00 diamond ring for only a $1.50 per week. Wright, Campbell and Ginder announced convenient evening hours to go along with its fine

Above: Cole's sign. *Image from Wikimedia Commons.*

Right: Philippe's. *Image from Wikimedia Commons.*

selection of stationery. Donavan & Seaman urged readers to "make it a diamond Christmas," while Brock and Company guaranteed "the perfect diamond" to their customer base.

Downtown restaurants assured hungry shoppers of a wide selection of great food. The Pacific Dining Car rigged out an old train coach as a formal, white tablecloth dining establishment. Magee's Kitchen featured a vast array of sandwiches and comfort foods. The Open Kitchen's down home cooking maintained its own loyal eaters. For snacks, Van de Kamp's Holland Bakery served mouthwatering homemade potato chips and cookies.

Since 1908, patrons had lined up at Cole's in the Pacific Electric Building on East Sixth Street for its famous French dip beef sandwich and a side pickle. Not to be outdone, Philippe's, which also opened in 1908, located on Alameda Street, contested Cole's claim of inventing the popular treat and retained its own substantial cadre of loyal followers.

The Grand Central Market, which opened in 1917 on the first floor of the Homer Laughlin Building, drew tourists and locals alike to its ninety stalls to sample a hodgepodge of ethnic foods, fresh vegetables, fruits, meats, prepared meals, baked goods and desserts, in addition to a selection of flowers, apparel and sundries. Bunker Hill residents hiked from their grand Victorian painted lady homes, paid a nominal toll and rode for 298 feet on the Angels Flight Funicular, the world's shortest railroad, to make their way to the market below for their shopping needs. Hourly workers scattered throughout downtown snapped up goodies for a snack, breakfast or lunch at their favorite booth.

The exterior of Grand Central Market on Broadway. *Courtesy of the Works Progress Administration.*

Stockbrokers, accountants, lawyers, oil executives and business executives jammed the upper floors of the city's growing number of high-rise buildings. Spring Street evolved into the Wall Street of the West. Financiers E.F. Hutton, D.H. Durst-Akim-Lambert, Logan & Bryan, First Securities, Frick, Martin & Company, William R. Staats, Banks Huntley, Commercial Mortgage, Corbin Oil Stocks and Merrill Lynch stood out among the dozens of dealers in stocks and bonds servicing the affluent. With the stock market soaring, blue chip stock American Telephone and Telegraph stood at a robust $131 per share, and U.S. Steel cost $118 per share. High-grade bonds paid more than a 4.0 percent interest, and more speculative investments offered even higher rates. Broker Howard G. Rath promoted a selection of aggressive financial vehicles, paying 6.5 to 7.5 percent interest.

Following the turn of the twentieth century, Los Angeles's commercial buildings rose skyward with each ensuing year. Developers opened the nine-story Pacific Electric building in 1904, with first-floor retail stores and office space on the upper floors. The six-story Italian Renaissance San Fernando followed in 1906 as a physician's cooperative communications exchange. The owners extended its height by two stories in 1911.

The city's first acknowledged skyscraper, the twelve-story Braly or Continental Building, emerged in 1908. Downtowners proclaimed it an architectural wonder. In 1924, the thirteen-story Commercial Exchange Building on Olive and Eighth Streets swelled the office landscape.

A host of banks provided for the financial needs of businesses and the public in 1924. The statuesque limestone façade, vaulted arches, stately pillars and marble floors of the Hellman Commercial Trust and Savings projected the perfect conservative image of stability. Unfortunately, Hellman Commercial ceased operations in 1928, and the Bank of America took over

Farmers and Merchants Bank, 1923. *Courtesy of the LAPL.*

the location. Eventually, the building morphed into the Majestic, a wedding, bar mitzvah, confirmation and special events venue in later years.

The Greek Revival Security and Trust Bank, situated at Fifth and Spring Streets, presented the classical dignity of a Hellenic temple. Its decorative exterior wrought iron sconces, giant columns, inlaid mosaic marble floors and an interior stained-glass window measuring fifty by one hundred feet cemented its reputation as a city landmark.

The handsome Farmers and Merchants Bank resembled a Roman temple, outfitted with ornate Corinthian columns. The Bank of Italy erected the palatial, neoclassical, Doric-columned, twelve-story Giannini Building on South Olive Street as a symbol of the trust its working-class customers could expect. In 1928, the Bank of Italy merged with its smaller rival, the Bank of America.

Equally impressive to the architecture of the neoclassical banks and financial houses was the world-famous downtown theater district. The depth and breadth of the "Broadway of the West's" offerings rivaled those of New York as the entertainment capital of America. In addition to the delight of the locals, thousands of tourists poured into the downtown to sample live theater, music hall performances, vaudeville shows, dance pavilion entertainment and silent movies.

The Million Dollar Theater, one of the first grand theaters in the country, opened in 1917 with the movie *The Silent Man*, starring cowboy star William S. Hart. Boasting 2,345 seats, the auditorium presented a December 24, 1924 circus extravaganza, the "Sawdust Ring," featuring performing monkeys, singing mules, trained elephants and other animal acts. The theater scheduled *Peter Pan*, starring Betty Bronson, to open the week after Christmas.

Million Dollar Theater building. *Image from Wikimedia.*

The Criterion, formerly known as the Kinema, opened on September 26, 1923, with the world premiere of Charlie Chaplin's *A Woman of Paris*. The theater then featured *Dante's Inferno*, with a complex plot combining elements from Dante Alighieri's poem with touches of Charles Dickens's *A Christmas Carol*.

Grauman's Metropolitan, the largest theater in the city, seated 3,500. The auditorium played the 105-minute-long *Romola*, starring the incomparable Gish sisters, Dorothy and Lillian, as well as headliners William Powell and Ronald Coleman. The owners later changed the name of the theater to the Paramount.

The Morosco staged a live three-act comedy, *It's a Boy*, and the Rialto ran with *Broken Laws*. The Philharmonic had performed Brahms's Symphony No. 1 the day prior.

Dozens of smaller theaters clustered in the Broadway district: Tally's showed Charlie Chaplin in *The Kid*; the Cameo, *Don't Marry for Money*; the Casino, Harry Carey in *Roaring Rails*; the California, an *Our Gang* comedy accompanied by the Carli Elinor Orchestra; the Lyceum, *Madonna of the Streets*; the Mission, *Age of Innocence*; the Optic, *Another Man's Wife*; the Regent, *Butterfly*; the Miller, *Christine of the Hungry Heart*; and Criangers Biltmore, *Merton of the Movies*. The city's entertainment district boasted that it contained more theaters than any other city in the country. With Warner Brothers' release of America's first talkie in 1927, *The Jazz Singer*, starring Al Jolson, movies, which were already enjoyed by millions, exploded in popularity, and the city's output of films ratcheted upward with the demand for more material.

The Roaring Twenties elevated Los Angeles's opulence astronomically, and hip upper-crusters dressed the part. Gentlemen wore suits and ties. Even blue-collar workers appeared dapper. The average Joe donned a hat—the bowler, Panama, boater, Homburg, gambler, newsboy cap or top hat for formal wear. Men completed their outfits with basic brown, black or tan tie-on shoes and even an occasional pair of two-toned shoes for sporty occasions.

The December 20, 1924 *Los Angeles Times* scattered menswear advertisements throughout the paper. Center city haberdasher Harris and Frank on Spring Street promoted $30.00 overcoats for the well-dressed male. Logan the Hatter advertised the prestigious Stetson line. Wood Brothers Hats publicized its huge selection. Young's Shoes stocked sizes to fit every foot, and B.H. Dyas, located on Seventh and Olive Streets, pushed motor robes for just $7.95. Department stores, including Hamburgers, Bullocks and J.W. Robinson, packed the paper with dozens of last-minute men's gift ideas.

TWYEFFORT, Inc.
580 5th AVENUE
NEW YORK

Left: A men's evening suit, 1925. *Courtesy of the Library of Congress.*

Right: Ladies' clothing styles, circa the 1920s. *Image from Wikimedia Commons.*

Distinctly clad, affluent men of the 1920s with the proper social connections joined the prestigious Jonathan Club on Figueroa Street or the California Club on Fifth Street. Both organizations excluded women and minorities from their membership. To quote the local adage: "The Jonathan Club ran the city; the California Club owned it."

Ladies came into their own during this golden age of fashion. Four years earlier, men had finally granted them the right to vote with the passage of the Nineteenth Amendment. Women strutted their stuff during the Roaring Twenties to demonstrate their flare and independence.

The typical flapper embraced the flat-chested La Garçonne style, featuring a straight-line—almost boyish—tunic skirt worn below the knee, usually at ankle length. Any lady worth her salt considered an outfit incomplete without the proper hat. The cloche, turban, bucket, beret or some form of wide-brim, floral-accented look coordinated nicely with the popular bobbed hairstyles. An evening on the town elicited beaded or feathered headbands to produce the vamp look—guaranteed to catch the eye of the opposite sex. Since free-spirited ladies often smoked, the modern woman toted a beaded purse for her makeup and cigarettes. Princess-, matinee- or opera-length pearl and tassel necklaces matched drop earrings to complete any outfit.

Dozens of tempting pre-Christmas advertisements from downtown retailers catered to the female buyer: G.H. Baker Shoes, the Unique's collection of $12.00 to $15.50 felt hats, Bedroll's six hundred dresses at half off, Colburn's furs, Vogue's fashionable designs, Jesberg's Walk-Over Shops' twenty-eight shades of hosiery, Myer Siegel's selection of coats at $19.95 and Harry Fink Company's collection of dance frocks. Owl Drug promoted a full page of perfumes, and department stores ensured plenty of other shopping options.

A plethora of variety stores rounded out downtown's appeal. Wiley B. Allen advertised Radiola radios and Wurlitzer organs. Barker Brothers Furniture promoted dining room chairs priced from $2.50 to $6.00 and matching tables from $5.00 to $30.00. The College Boot Shop, Parmelee and Dohrman's House of Housewares, Arnold Ross Luggage, Berkeley Company Victrolas, A.G. Spaulding and Cline & Cline Sporting Goods all publicized their wares for Christmas.

Store windows glowed with red and green lights and tiny reindeer pulling sleds. Industrious elves at workbenches tapped out toys, and mini-sized Christmas trees, bedecked with ornaments, sparkled and flickered. Children lined up inside the department stores to present their lists of wants to Santa. Salvation Army volunteers on the streets collected money in kettles for the needy. The spirit of gift-giving warmed the hearts of shoppers and merchants alike.

People loved to shop downtown. Women dressed in their Sunday finest, and men wore suits and ties. On the Saturday before Christmas, last-minute buyers packed the stores in search of the perfect gift.

In addition to the newspaper's gift-giving ideas, Dr. G.W. Fuller advanced his services as a specialist in the cure of piles. Dr. Zimmerman offered free dental examinations while employing the latest piece of equipment: the X-ray machine. Mackey Business College provided a list of available secretarial courses for the winter session.

The City of Angels, like New York in the East and Chicago in the Midwest, percolated with activity, dominating its western rival cities in sheer size as the center of finance, entertainment, shopping and the arts.

Philippe's lunch rush. *Image from Wikimedia Commons.*

The sweet aroma of money swirled through Los Angeles. The population explosion, the rip-roaring economy and plans for the construction of important buildings, such as the new city hall and a state-of-the-art public library, signaled to visionary entrepreneurs the vast opportunities available to those with the gumption to act.

With thousands gravitating to Los Angeles's downtown area for business, government, sports, shopping, medical care, entertainment and restaurants, the Queen City's demand for new hotels to house visitors grew obvious.

Recent advancements in the production of steel beams and reinforced concrete girders had supplied the materials necessary to build taller, safer and stronger buildings. Revised government codes permitted structures to climb above 150 feet in elevation. Architects floated modern designs that accommodated the increased height allowances, birthing modern skyscrapers with classical Renaissance Revival façades. Los Angeles, like its cousins New York and Chicago, had initiated a race to construct monster high-rises, aiming toward the clouds.

The magnificent Spanish-Italian Revival Los Angeles Biltmore Hotel, overlooking Pershing Park, opened on October 2, 1923, to rave reviews. The eleven-story, 1,500-room colossus covered half a city block on South Grand Avenue. The Biltmore debuted as the largest hotel west of Chicago. Prior to its opening, the still-popular Alexandria, built in 1906 and expanded in 1911, stood out as downtown Los Angeles's premier hotel.

The Biltmore's spectacular frescos and murals, its carved fountains, oak-paneled walls, crystal chandeliers and beamed ceilings elevated the hotel to become the city's finest, as well as its largest, hotel. The new establishment set the benchmark by which all future commercial and residential buildings would be measured.

To satisfy the growing demand for rooms, other hotels developed, expanded and remodeled. The South Main Street–Fifth Street downtown corridor had evolved into the "hotel district."

Any new entry into the field required a top-notch design, strong management and excellent service to keep up with the competition. The 215-room Baltimore; 360-room King Edward; 160-room Van Nuys; 555-room Clark; 264-room, twelve-story Hotel Stowell; the smaller Hayward on West Sixth Street; and the Hotel Alexandria on Spring Street maintained high occupancy levels. The owners of the Beaux-Arts Rosslyn and Rosslyn Annex, a mammoth hotel containing 1,100 rooms and 800 baths, located

The Biltmore Hotel, Los Angeles, 1943. *Courtesy of the Automobile Club of Southern California, digitally reproduced by the University of Southern California Digital Archive.*

Rosslyn Hotels. *Image from Wikimedia Commons.*

on Fifth and Main Streets, promoted a comfortable and clean night's stay at a reasonable price. The city's lodging industry glittered with promise and offered a strong pathway to success.

Veteran hotelier William Banks Hammer grasped the potential for additional mid-priced, quality hotel space along the lines of the Rosslyn's formula. The upstream economic movement of the Roaring Twenties, the growing need for additional space and an available and ideal downtown location created a Goldilocks moment. The time for action had come—*carpe diem*.

Hammer formed a consortium of movers and shakers to finance a fourteen-floor, seven-hundred-room hotel with a prime location at 640 South Main Street, an underutilized spot. The group wagered that the project would throw off a significant profit. William Banks Hammer became the president of the corporation. Partner Robert H. Schops took over the role of vice-president, and partner Charles L. Dix served as the secretary-treasurer.

Originally, Hammer intended to call the hotel the "Metropolitan," but after some give and take, he opted to name it after London's spectacular eight-hundred-room Cecil Hotel, constructed in 1896 along the River Thames.

Hotel Cecil (*left*) on the River Thames in London. *Courtesy of the Library of Congress.*

The investors hired top-notch Pomona College graduate Loy Lester Smith as architect to draw up plans for a Renaissance Revival, Beaux-Arts–style, 170,000-square-foot building.[1] Hammer brought in W.W. Paden and the firm of Weymouth Crowell as the general contractor for the $1,000,000 budgeted hotel. The banks and investors liked the project. The total cost, which included salaries, supplies, furnishings and overruns, probably totaled closer to $2,500,000 (approximately $37,134,000 today).

Hammer's artistic team performed with the skill and precision of Greece's great classical sculptor Phidias, who carved the gold and ivory statue of Athena at the Parthenon, a colossus that measured more than thirty-seven feet in height. The lines of the goddess's armor, her flowing dress, carved shield, helmet and spear—all clad in gold—approached perfection. Her ivory face radiated an ethereal beauty. Like Phideas had done more than 2,500 years before, Smith, Paden and Hammer imbued the Cecil with the regal grace and strength of the goddess Athena.

Marble pillars set off architect Smith's formal entryway, leading into a T-shaped lobby—the Cecil's pièce de résistance—the signature expression of the Roaring Twenties' prosperity. Its special touches included terrazzo

Opposite: An architectural sketch of Hotel Metropolitan/Cecil by L.L. Smith. Front elevation. *Courtesy of the City of Los Angeles.*

Above: The front entryway of the Cecil Hotel. *Image from the Historical-Cultural Monument application, City of Los Angeles.*

floors highlighted with an inlaid geometric mosaic, decorative wrought iron sconces, a grand staircase to the second-floor mezzanine, two backlit art-glass skylights, Art Deco chandeliers, a circular wooden clock with Roman numerals perched above the reservation desk, potted palm trees and discretely positioned alabaster statues of Greek goddesses draped in flowing gowns tucked in alcoves. These exclusive details delivered the important trappings people wanted and expected from a first-class hotel.

Giant signs measuring seventy feet in height on the northwest and southwest corners promoted the hotel's name. Raised gold letters reading "Cecil Hotel" greeted guests entering through the front doorway.

The hotel numbered its fourteen floors 1 through 15, skipping unlucky 13 per the custom of the day. One hundred truckloads containing more than four thousand specially made pieces of furniture, almost all constructed in California, arrived through the Cecil's doors in the weeks prior to its opening. Barker Brothers produced everything, with the exception of the overstuffed pieces manufactured by Roberts-Cohen Company of Huntington Park. The makers had produced each item to reinforce Smith's vision of dignity.

The lobby's walnut and red leather, Spanish-style chairs amplified the interior's classic feel. The mezzanine's comfortable reed furniture balanced the formality of the first floor.

The bedrooms included Windsor-style furniture designed for comfort and fit, wrought iron lamps with hand-painted parchment shades, fitted mattresses on double-decked springs and pillows stuffed with goose and duck down feathers to satisfy the discerning tastes of the time.

Barker Brothers demonstrated its appreciation for the large furniture contract with an impressive advertisement in the December 20, 1924 *Los Angeles Times*:

> [Congratulations to] *the Cecil Hotel and acknowledging the opportunity (through providing the furnishings) of sharing in the creative activities which have contributed to the successful opening of this splendid addition to the downtown hostelries of Los Angeles.*
>
> ## COMPLETELY UP-TO-DATE
> ## COMPLETELY COMFORTABLE
>
> *The furnishing scheme of the Cecil was planned with a view to giving unstinted comfort and contentment to the guests who are to sojourn beneath its roof.*
>
> ### BARKER BROTHERS
> *Complete Furnishers of Successful Homes, Hotels, All Public Buildings Broadway Between Seventh and Eighth*

On December 20, the *Los Angeles Times* reported that the German government had released Adolf Hitler from Landsberg Prison under a general amnesty program. Hitler had served 264 days of a five-year sentence for treason following the famed Munich Beer Hall Putsch, the Nazi Party's failed attempt to overthrow the government. While jailed, Hitler penned *Mein Kampf* (*My Struggle*) with the assistance of Rudolf Hess. On a lighter note, the newspaper announced a sellout of the upcoming Notre Dame–Stanford Rose Bowl football game.

Norman Shelby, better known as Kid McCoy, stood before a jury in his final defense for the murder of his girlfriend Theresa Mors and a separate shooting and robbery in an antique shop. The ten-time-wedded, flat-broke, former middleweight boxing champion appeared mentally unhinged. Addicted to booze and on the skids, the fallen hero received a sympathetic

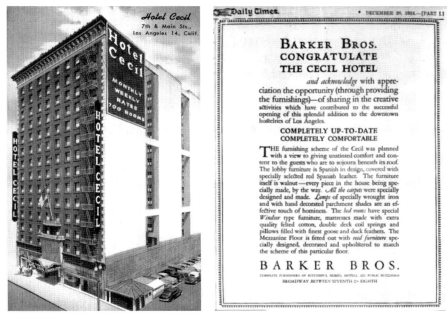

Left: A postcard view of Cecil Hotel. *Author's collection.*

Right: "Barker Bros. Congratulate the Cecil Hotel." *Image from the* Daily Times, *December 1924.*

hearing by a panel of his peers. In a compromise verdict, the tribunal convicted him of manslaughter rather than first-degree murder. The court sentenced him to a ten-year term at San Quentin. Additionally, in the boxing scene, Abe Goldstein lost his bantamweight title to Eddie Martin, and Jack Dempsey's promoters floated a match with Chilean Romero Rojas, a fight that never took place.

An advertisement on that same day in December appeared in the *Los Angeles Times*, announcing the grand opening of the Cecil. The hotel offered three hundred of its seven hundred rooms with communal showers and baths for $1.50 per night, two hundred with a private toilet for $2.00 and two hundred with a private toilet and a bath for $2.50. The hotel provided additional discounts for monthly rentals. The Cecil's investors had constructed a state-of-the-art hotel for the times. The only shortsighted design flaw involved the four hundred rooms that lacked both a private toilet and bath.

Reasonable prices, a convenient location near the train station and proximity to restaurants, theaters, shopping venues, hospitals and financial services enhanced the strong demand for nightly rooms at the Cecil and led

Left: An advertisement for the opening of the Cecil Hotel, 1924. *Courtesy of the City of Los Angeles.*

Above: The unique ceiling lanterns of the Cecil Hotel. *Image from the Historical-Cultural Monument application, City of Los Angeles.*

to an excellent early financial performance. The Hotel Cecil thrived on a mix of permanent residents, middle-class tourists and Angelenos out for an evening's adventure.

Right from the start, the rooms were filled. Management smiled at its good fortune. In November 1925, Hammer, who owned the Oasis Hotel in Palm Springs in addition to the Cecil, expanded his portfolio. He inked a $200,000 lease for the under-construction Community Hotel in Brawley at the southern tip of California. He also purchased another small establishment known as the Ajax. The Hammer group, like most of Los Angeles's entrepreneurs, appeared to be on a roll, dancing to the beat of a swirling upward-moving economy.

The public considered the Cecil a prestige property—a place to see and be seen. The December 10, 1926 issue of the *Fresno News* announced that local citizens Mr. and Mrs. E. Stephenson, H. Ling, Gladstone Reed and B.F. Francis had recently visited Los Angeles and stayed at the Cecil. With the hotel's occupancy statistics on fire, William Banks Hammer celebrated his shrewd acquisition.

Sometime in 1928, award-winning artist Lydia Herman loaned her painting of Morro Rock in San Luis Obispo to hang in the Cecil's lobby, an oil admired by many of the guests. In 1931, the painter departed from California to Hawaii and took her artwork with her.

Like with most hotels, the name of the Cecil turned up in the papers for minor imbroglios. In 1925, with the Volstead Act in full force, making alcohol illegal, a twenty-three-year-old named Mrs. Wall hosted a drinking party in her room at the Cecil. The police raided the shindig after other occupants complained about the noise. The officers might have overlooked the infraction, but they arrested Mrs. Wall for serving liquor to a twenty-year-old minor.

On January 22, 1927, fifty-two-year-old Percy Ormond Cook, a former real estate dealer from Providence, Rhode Island, shot himself in his room at the Cecil. He had spent $40,000 over the past several months, trying to forget his wife and son, from whom he had separated. He reputedly owned the Willard Apartments in Hollywood, and his son attended Harvard University. Brooding over his loneliness, he penned a suicide note, which read: "Money cannot buy you happiness. I have tried it and found it cannot be done. I have lost my wife, my son and my home, and I am doing the only thing left for me to do." Cook died in an ambulance on his way to the general hospital and may have been the hotel's first confirmed suicide.

Later that year, the police arrested petty crook John Croneur at the Cecil. Described by the papers as a "suave and mild-mannered Slavonian," Croneur had pilfered a diamond hairpin at the Rosslyn Hotel. The authorities chased the thief out of the Rosslyn, through the Hayward Hotel and into the Cecil, where they captured him.

Thirty-three-year-old San Francisco native Dorothy Richardson wandered aimlessly through the halls of the Cecil for three days. Guests and management took little notice of her odd behavior until she created a scene on April 27, 1929. Mrs. Richardson collapsed on the floor near the lobby stairs. Witnesses assumed she had died. A call from management brought an ambulance, which delivered her to a nearby hospital. The recent, unexpected death of her husband had unhinged her, and she attempted to end her life with an overdose of barbiturates. She survived.

During the late 1920s, police arrested Cecil resident George Ford, a high-profile morphine and opium dealer, during a sting operation at the nearby Astor Hotel. The authorities confiscated $10,000 (about $145,000 today) in cash and drugs.

In another incident, an ambulance picked up an elderly resident at the Cecil in "peril of death." He had imbibed poisoned liquor that killed three other men.

These minor glitches did little to quell the optimism of the owners. Hotel management expected problems as a normal part of the operation, but the rewards far exceeded the snags.

The Roaring Twenties boosted the city's overall sense of prosperity to the nth degree, and downtown Los Angeles sucked in the euphoria. New

Rosslyn Annex Hotel. *Image from Wikimedia Commons.*

construction, the expanding movie industry, a soaring stock market, dozens of new business projects and government expansion prophesied years of continued progress. The twenty-eight-story city hall, completed in April 1928, provided concrete proof of the ever-expanding skyline and the confidence in the stability of the economy. Business at the Cecil could hardly have been better.

Whether intoxicated from the jolt of a shot of bootleg gin, frolicking like the flappers and their beaus to the beat of the Charleston or joining the herds of impetuous bulls boosting the stock market, a rush of chutzpah bathed downtown. Los Angeles, like the rest of the country, lived in a world of dreams—a royal straight flush of arrogance. On September 3, 1929, the Dow Jones market average struck the astronomical high of 381.1. Could life be any better?

2

THE DEPRESSION AND HARD TIMES

The world can be a brutal master. Fate often mocks the hubris of the human race. Just when we sit back in our easy chair to relish our fruits from years of hard work, a tornado can strike and obliterate all that we have achieved. Like the little pig who built his house of straw, a wolf can huff and puff and blow your house down with a couple deep breaths. The fragile crystal goblet we created, when dropped to the floor, can shatter into dozens of worthless shards.

On October 23, 1929, the economy's strength appeared unshakable, as firm as the rock of Gibraltar. In actuality, the overinflated economy stood poised for a massive correction. The very next day, October 24, "Black Thursday," the stock market exploded like the hydrogen-filled *Hindenburg* a few years later. Edgy investors dumped 12,894,680 shares of stock, the greatest number ever traded to that date.

A *Los Angeles Times* cartoon depicted a wise bull watching a speculator calf run amok in a panic. The headline warned the calf not to join the stampede. The newspaper's advice proved wrong. Five days later, on "Black Tuesday," nearly 17 million shares of stock sold at bargain-basement pricing, wiping out thousands of investors. Greedy fools had borrowed money on margin in hopes of making a quick buck in a raging market. Those bets were lost in a big way. Bankrupt investors leaped from tall buildings in despair rather than face the humiliation of bankruptcy or life on the streets.

The economy had imploded through what maverick Harvard professor Robert Z. Ripley called "prestidigitation, double-shuffling, honey-fueling and skullduggery." The next decade would be a cesspool of sorrow for most of the country.

On November 13, 1929, the Dow had slumped to 199. By July 9, 1932, stocks had plummeted 91 percent in value from their highs to 41.63. "Brother Can You Spare a Dime" became one of the nation's top musical hits—for good reason. Folks weren't dancing the Charleston any longer.

With each week, the economy slid from poor to atrocious. The entire country had catapulted into the Great Depression. Hiring for jobs slowed to a standstill. Families disintegrated, chewed up and spit out by the poverty of the 1930s. Good people sat on the edge of starvation. President Herbert Hoover urged the country to remain calm and "hold the course," but his advice leaked water. There was no "chicken in every pot" as promised during his 1928 campaign against Democrat contender Al Smith.

Even wily bankers had succumbed to the promise of endless riches. Assets declined in direct proportion to the degree of investment. Frightened depositors lined up in droves outside these temples of mammon to retrieve their cash. Many lost everything when the Depression shuttered 744 banks throughout the country during the first ten months of the financial holocaust. In 1932, the Depression erased 2,500 banks, with another 4,000 succumbing the following year.

As industrial production declined by nearly 50 percent, jobs evaporated. Hardworking people lined up at soup kitchens or bread lines in search of a bite to eat. By 1933, unemployment had escalated to 25 percent.

The United States became a sad place, and Skid Row was one of its saddest subsidiaries. Dispossessed of their homes by storms in the Dust Bowl and economic hardships, thousands of unfortunates gravitated to the West Coast for its warm weather and jobs that no longer existed.

One downcast soul stood by the curb at the corner of Seventh and Main Streets, hoping for a handout as he sang the old ditty, "If money talks, it ain't on speaking terms with me." The coins in his hat came few and far between; most of his brothers and sisters rowed upstream in that same sinking boat.

The Cecil Hotel sat on the edge of the fifty-block area politically known as Central City East, but the locals called it Skid Row. Third Street bordered the area to the north, Seventh Street to the south, Alameda Street to the east and Main Street to the west.[2] The Depression punished this poor sector of Los Angeles with impunity. As many as ten thousand homeless slept on the streets in and around its limits. Beggars staked out every corner, while thieves and pickpockets scared away law-abiding shoppers. Soup kitchens replaced

A common Depression-era scene. *Courtesy of the Library of Congress.*

white-tablecloth restaurants. Tony retail stores closed their businesses, leaving vacant storefronts in their wake.

Although the Depression ended for the rest of the country sometime around 1939 or 1940, Skid Row and the bordering district continued to suffer the scourge of poverty and homelessness for decades to follow.

The Cecil's economics crashed even more than the rest of the downtown. The quantity and quality of the hotel's clientele took a nosedive. Furnishings, bedding, paint and fixtures requiring routine repair or replacement remained in use. The lobby filled with drifters, grifters, junkies, runaways and riffraff. The hotel became a rendezvous point for drugs, prostitution and adultery. The times, the economy and the subpar caliber of the occupants cooked up a recipe for disaster in and around Skid Row. In short order, bad things happened, and the police found themselves visiting the Cecil on a routine basis.

Forty-four-year-old Frank Everett Lindsey, a suspect in the murder of his wife, who was also accused of abducting eleven-year-old Pearl Grant, spent the night of September 9, 1930, at the Cecil. The police arrested Lindsey on

October 18 on a charge of second-degree kidnapping. Under questioning, Grant recanted his accusation and said no murdered wife actually existed. The authorities dropped all charges and released Lindsey.

On December 1, 1930, officers arrested resident and petty criminal Mickey McDonald, also known as Vernon Charles Smith, on charges of kiting a bogus check for $24.75 at F.W. Alley Jewelry. He also conned Tubbs Sporting Goods and Triangle Shoes into granting him false credit for merchandise.

Nineteen-year-old Boyd Hanson's car struck that of Cecil resident Roy E. Smith on January 21, 1931. Smith died in the accident. The authorities cleared Boyd of any wrongdoing.

While retailers in the neighborhood closed, the Cecil struggled through the decade, battling to maintain solvency and pay lenders for borrowed funds. Regardless of how diligently management worked, deadly events occurred, and the hotel's cash flow fell.

On November 19, 1931, the Cecil recorded its first known suicide in the 1930s. During a routine room check, a cleaning lady with just a few months on the job rapped on a guest's door and announced, "Service." Receiving no answer, she assumed the room was empty and entered with her passkey. The maid discovered the gray and lifeless body of fully clothed forty-six-year-old W.K. Norton of Manhattan Beach lying on the bed. The employee called the manager, who immediately summoned the police.

The decedent had checked into the Cecil under the alias James Willys of Chicago six days earlier, but bank checks in his pocket indicated his true identity. He killed himself using poison capsules, several of which were discovered in his vest pocket. Investigators found no signs of foul play. Norton's wife indicated that her husband had suffered from despondency over economic reverses. "The Depression had done him in."

In July 1934, former army medical sergeant fifty-three-year-old Louis D. Borden slashed his own throat with a razor in a bloody mess. The victim left a suicide note citing ill health as the reason for his suicide. In a separate letter, Borden requested that Edna Hasoner of Post Office Box 664 in Edmonds, Washington, become the "sole survivor of the little I leave."

Throughout the 1930s, the Cecil catered to a mixed lower-rung clientele, accepting any and all who had the few dollars required for a room. Tourists on a budget from around the world visited the Cecil for a few days of business or pleasure. Folks who had fallen on hard times during the Depression stayed on as permanent or long-term residents.

An elderly, retired U.S. Cavalry soldier who had once served with General George Armstrong Custer of Little Bighorn fame regaled all those who had the time with a repertoire of stories about his days in the service. He remained a resident for six months.

Lethal coincidences continued with alarming frequency around the hotel. In an automobile accident, Louis G. Mathausen's vehicle struck and killed pedestrian Virgil Tallman, age thirty, a Cecil resident.

In 1937, Grace E. Magro, age twenty-five, died at the Georgia Receiving Hospital after jumping or falling from her hotel room onto the telephone wires. Her companion M.W. Madison, a twenty-six-year-old sailor from the USS *Virginia*, claimed he had been sleeping and could provide no explanation for what happened. The manager of the hotel, J.B. Read Jr., corroborated the plausibility of Madison's story, and no charges were filed.

In 1938, thirty-five-year-old Roy Thompson, a fireman with the marine corps, jumped to his death from the window of room 1431 and crashed onto the skylight of the neighboring building. Los Angeles detectives Clark and Hill notified his brother W.E. Thompson of Port Arthur, Texas, of Roy's untimely death.

On April 15 the same year, police arrested and jailed resident Kenneth Class, age thirty-nine, a small-timer, for forgery and passing off bad checks.

The mysterious deaths and arrests escalated like the pile of victims from the Spanish flu virus of 1918, which had been spread from person to person by careless sneezes. An elderly male resident shot himself at Westlake Park, and a female drowned in the ocean. Police arrested a teenage stickup bandit at the hotel with a note reading: "You are covered. Open that cash register and shell out. No tricks or else."[3]

A woman named Dorothy January posted an advertisement for childcare. A male respondent came to her hotel room, entered and choked her into submission. He then took her purse and escaped with forty dollars.

Robert Marcus Burgunder came from an outstanding family in Seattle, Washington. The community held his attorney father in high esteem. However, even as a child, Robert acted oddly. In high school, he exhibited a perverse interest in crime and his father's felony cases.

In 1936, nineteen-year-old Burgunder donned a Boy Scout uniform and held up a drugstore for fourteen dollars. He received a sentence at a reform school as punishment. Once paroled, he attended a teacher's college, where he received good grades without studying, but his out-of-whack behavior continued. His public speaking teacher remembered the outline for a speech he had written about committing the perfect murder. Robert's actions concerned his father, his teachers and his classmates.

On May 1, 1939, twenty-two-year-old Burgunder wandered into a Phoenix, Arizona car dealership and introduced himself as Bob Lesser, a resident of the Cecil Hotel in Los Angeles. He asked two salesmen to take him for a test drive. Police later discovered the bodies of the salesmen in the desert near Maricopa. The killer had tied the legs of the deceased with their own belts before shooting them.

The authorities arrested the nervous and guilty-acting Burgunder in Johnson City, Tennessee, with a pistol in his possession. The legal system tried, convicted and eventually executed him in the gas chamber on August 9, 1940.

In January 1940, depressed teacher Dorothy Steiger, age forty-five, ingested poison while staying at the Cecil. An ambulance delivered her to a local hospital "near death." She passed away the following day and received burial at the Evergreen Memorial Park and Mausoleum in Riverside. Interestingly, the hotel's first Alcoholics Anonymous meetings took place the same year.

The Cecil drew trouble like honey attracted bears, enticing cheating couples, assignations with prostitutes and drug deals. Dozens of cases never hit the newspapers.

The better classes of guests defected to the upscale Biltmore, the Alexandria or one of the newer hotels in the suburbs. The Cecil's salad days had ended long ago. Travelers and residents alike considered the hotel a second-rate Sally. The 1940s proved to be even worse than the 1930s.

A café manager who lived at the hotel died in a gunfight with the bartender at the nearby Waldorf Cellar Bar. The killer and the victim had once been best childhood friends.

As the economy throttled the Cecil's shaky finances, the Albert Group stepped in and took over the hotel in 1941. Both tenants and staff viewed the change in management positively. Mrs. Dudley Albert ran the company as president, and her son J.H. Albert served as secretary treasurer. The Albert chain ran an impressive portfolio of hotels along the western states, including the Hotel McCoy in El Paso, the seven-story Hotel Jefferson in Phoenix (at one time, the tallest building in Arizona), the four-story Hotel Southern in San Diego, the Morrison Post at the corner of Pico and Hope Streets and the Californian on Sixth Street in downtown Los Angeles.

The Albert family specialized in updating historic properties. To turn around the Cecil, the new owners implemented a series of cosmetic and service improvements. The residents and staff appreciated the remodeling, but the changes barely slowed the hotel's downward spiral.

With its difficulty in attracting boarders, the Cecil advertised below-market rates of only one dollar per day or six dollars per week in the *Phoenix Republic* to attract an out-of-town tourist clientele.

In September 1944, nineteen-year-old Dorothy Jean Purcell awoke in the middle of the night with severe stomach cramps. She slipped into the bathroom to avoid waking her lover, thirty-eight-year-old shoe salesman Ben Levine. To her shock, she delivered a baby boy. She claimed to have been unaware of her pregnancy. Groggy, confused and thinking the infant stillborn, she threw him out the window, down twelve stories, to the roof of the next door building without ever waking Levine. A report of the incident to the police brought a squad of investigators. Following a room-by-room search, the police arrested Miss Purcell and took her to the General Hospital Prison Ward.

An autopsy conducted by Dr. Frank R. Webb of the coroner's office discovered air in the child's lungs at the time of death, proof the infant had been alive. This led to a formal charge of murder. At the inquest, police officer Stewart Jones testified that Purcell and her boyfriend had spent several days at the Cecil prior to the incident. A team of alienists, today known as psychologists, testified that she had been temporarily insane at the time of the murder but of sound mind afterward. Based on the testimony of the experts, the jury acquitted Purcell of murder, with one member of the panel describing the case as "almost beyond belief." However, the court sentenced her to time at a psychiatric hospital for further evaluation. Once released, she married a navy veteran and died in 2000 at the age of seventy-five.

Far stranger and darker episodes would mar the Cecil's reputation in the ensuing years.

THE BLACK DAHLIA MURDER

T he Black Dahlia murder represented one of the most elusive and brutal homicides in the history of crime, and at least one witness tied the butchery to the Cecil Hotel.

Elizabeth, "Bette" or "Betty," Short was born in Hyde Park, Massachusetts, on July 29, 1924, the third of Phoebe and Cleo Short's five daughters. She grew up in Medford, a suburb of Boston, where her father built miniature golf courses. When the Depression hit, the Short family's finances tanked. Cleo's golf business evaporated, sucking up his income and leaving him with a stack of unpaid bills.

Despondency crushed Mr. Short. With an outlook bordering on the hopeless, he abandoned his car on the Charlestown Bridge and disappeared, leaving his wife and children to fend for themselves. The family assumed he had killed himself. Elizabeth's mother located a position as a bookkeeper and struggled to make ends meet. To cut expenses, she moved her daughters from their home into a cramped apartment.

As a teenager, Elizabeth escaped from poverty into the imaginary world of Hollywood whenever her mother could obtain free tickets to the theater. She dreamed of becoming a movie star like her idols, Ingrid Bergman, Irene Dunne and Katharine Hepburn. She possessed the looks. Even as a young girl, neighbors described her as "that black Irish beauty."

Troubled by asthma and bronchitis, Elizabeth required surgery at the age of fifteen to help with her breathing. Her doctor suggested she go south to warmer weather during the winter months. She dropped out of high school after her sophomore year and went to Miami for the next three winters to work as a waitress.

In 1942, the Short family discovered that Cleo had not died by suicide. Phoebe received a letter of apology from her husband. He had started a new life in Vallejo, California. Cleo invited his daughter Elizabeth to visit. With dreams of stardom floating through her brain, the eighteen-year-old traveled west to spend time with her father, whom she had not seen since she was six years old. The reunion quickly soured. Elizabeth considered her father old-fashioned. He disapproved of her late hours, dates with servicemen and modern ways. Cleo ordered his daughter to vacate.

Elizabeth Short. *Image from the LAPD's files.*

Elizabeth left and found a job at Camp Cooke, now called Vandenberg Air Force Base, located outside the city of Lompoc. Although the troops considered her a loner and a "tease," the boys took to her looks and voted her "Camp Cutie of the Week."

In 1943, Elizabeth, or Bette as her friends called her, moved to Santa Barbara, where the police arrested her on September 23 for underage drinking. The authorities mandated her to return to Medford, but she relocated to Florida, where she met Major Matthew Gordon, a decorated army air force officer.

Major Matthew Michael Gordon Jr. *Image from Wikimedia Commons.*

Short told friends that Gordon had proposed while healing from the effects of a plane crash in India. She accepted. Unfortunately, her fiancé died in a second crash on August 10, 1945, the week before Japan's surrender.

Elizabeth returned to Los Angeles in July 1946 to visit Lieutenant Joseph Fickling, a friend she knew from Florida. She opted to stay in Southern California, catching part-time jobs as a waitress in the hopes of finding a modeling gig—or better yet, discovery by a film producer. Like thousands of young women seeking fame and fortune as a Hollywood leading lady, the movie industry meat grinder chewed her up and crushed her dreams.

Elizabeth survived on menial jobs and the kindness of strangers. She moved in with other women to split the rent of a dollar or two per day. Her roommates complained of her inability to come up with her fair share on time. When she borrowed nail polish or cosmetics, she rarely replaced what she had used. Before dates, she hogged the mirror as she styled her hair, painted her nails and colored her lips. Bette looked perfect in every way except for the obvious black cavities in her mouth. Since she lacked the money to visit a dentist, she filled the holes with wax. One critic nicknamed her "'Miss Hoity Toity.' She always thought she was better than the rest of us."

Supposedly, a serviceman coined the name "Black Dahlia" based on Elizabeth Short's good looks, blue eyes and raven black hair. When he spotted her sipping a coke through a straw at his favorite soda fountain in Long Beach, he thought about the 1946 movie *The Blue Dahlia*, which starred Alan Ladd and Veronica Lake. He merely altered the title to fit her dark-black, bouffant-style hair, red lips and cream-colored skin.

On January 9, 1947, Robert "Red" Manley, a twenty-five-year-old married salesman with a crush on Bette, dropped her off at 6:30 p.m. at the Biltmore Hotel entrance on 506 South Grand Street, several blocks from the Cecil. She told Red that she intended to meet her sister Virginia at the hotel. A member of the Biltmore staff recalled seeing her make a call on the lobby telephone. Allegedly, other patrons spotted her at the Crown Grill Cocktail Lounge on Olive Street, a few blocks from the Biltmore, on the same date.

Ken Schessler, the author of *This Is Hollywood*, claimed that witnesses had seen Elizabeth Short with two sailors and another woman at the Cecil and the Dugout Bar next door, two of her favorite hangouts.

The Biltmore Hotel lobby. *Image from Wikimedia Commons.*

Police officer Meryl McBride saw Elizabeth Short having a drink at the Cecil Hotel bar. She testified to speaking with the girl shortly before her disappearance. On the afternoon of January 14, Elizabeth "came running up to me while I was on my patrol beat near the Greyhound Bus Depot. She was sobbing and frightened. She told me that she had just run into a former boyfriend at a bar down the street, and he had threatened to kill her if he found her with another man. I walked her back to the bar. We got her purse, but the man was gone."

"Officer McBride resumed her foot patrol duties, and about an hour later, Elizabeth Short exited another bar with 'two men and a woman.'" The policewoman confirmed "her positive identification" and said that one of the bars had been at the Cecil.[4] McBride may have been the last person to report a sighting of Elizabeth Short while she was still alive.

Around 10:30 a.m. on January 15, Betty Bersinger, accompanied by her three-year-old child, headed toward the shoe repair shop. As she passed along South Norton Avenue, midway between Coliseum and West Thirty-Ninth Streets, she spotted a chalk-white, broken mannequin lying off to the side in a vacant lot. When she looked more closely, she realized it wasn't a mannequin; rather, it was a face-up nude body, severed at the waist, staring up at her. Mrs. Bersinger gasped, took in a deep breath to capture her composure and scurried to a nearby house to telephone the police.

Officers Frank Perkins and Will Fitzgerald arrived in minutes and immediately summoned backup. Detective Sergeant Jesse Haskins arrived at 11:18 a.m. Droves of investigators flocked to the scene, followed by a slew of reporters and photographers. No one could recall seeing anything so bizarre.

The two segments of the severed corpse lay separated by an almost-one-foot space. The killer had drained the victim's blood and washed the body to create an unnatural, white, plastic appearance. The woman's intestines lay beneath her buttocks. Geometric slices of flesh from her thighs and left breast had been inserted in her vagina. The victim's right breast had been removed in its entirety with surgical skill. The woman's face, cut from ear to ear, produced the horrific effect

Betty Bersinger. *Image from the Herald Examiner, 1947.*

known as a Glasgow or Chelsea smile. With artistic precision, the culprit had posed both her arms above her head, each bent at a forty-five-degree angle away from the body. The right arm also slanted at a ninety-degree angle at the elbow. The killer spread her legs wide. No clothing lay near the nude body—only an empty fifty-pound paper cement bag.

Police soon arrived at the crime scene in en masse. Even hardened detectives cringed at the macabre sight. Around 2:00 p.m., a hearse arrived and delivered the chopped-up corpse to the Los Angeles City Morgue. Police later located the victim's discarded purse and shoes in a trash bin near 1136 Crenshaw Boulevard.

The FBI identified the victim from fingerprints taken from her underage drinking arrest and an employment application from Camp Cooke—she was twenty-two-year-old Elizabeth Short. She would have stood about five feet, five inches tall and weighed around 115 pounds.

Elizabeth Short had last been seen at the Cecil and Biltmore Hotels wearing a black suit; a beige, full-length, collarless coat; a fluffy white blouse; nylon stockings; and black suede high heels, and she had been carrying a black plastic purse.

As a result of the autopsy, medical examiner Dr. Frederic Newbarr described "a horrific and painful death."

> *This young woman was trussed and bound by her hands and feet, was tortured initially by minor cuts to her body and to her private parts, then cutting away her pubic hairs, which he later would insert into her vagina. She was then beaten about her entire body. She was forced to eat her own or their fecal excrement. Finally, she was beaten to death, and her face and body were viciously lacerated and defiled. The killer(s) cut large pieces of flesh from her body, which they inserted in her vagina and rectum. Her killer sliced her mouth from ear to ear into a bloody grin, lacerated her breasts and cleanly bisected her body.…The body was drained of blood— exsanguination—and her hair and body were washed clean.[5]*

Short's wrists showed rope burns, and her remaining breast had been burned by lit cigarettes.

The police recognized that the killer possessed the surgical skill of a doctor, combined with the sadism of Marquis de Sade. The transection of the lumbar spine, known medically as a hemicorporectomy, demanded advanced knowledge of human anatomy. The coroner explained: "The trunk is completely severed by an incision through the abdomen, severing the intestine at the duodenum and passing through the intervertebral disk between the second and third lumbar vertebra."[6]

The autopsy revealed another strange factor: Elizabeth Short was born with androgen insensitivity syndrome. Women with AIS can look and feel like women, even though they possess XY chromosomes and may have tiny testes. They can never bear children and generally lack a fully developed uterus. In Elizabeth's case, the doctor surmised she would have had difficulty having penetrative sex.

The mysterious Black Dahlia murder consumed the public for months. Page-one coverage of the crime continued in the *Los Angeles Times* for thirty-one days in a row.

Within days, the *Los Angeles Examiner*'s city editor Bill Robertson received a call from a "soft, sly voice" promising to send some of Short's effects.[7] Two days later, Robertson, along with Captain Jack Donahue of the LAPD and other law enforcement detectives, opened a package at the Los Angeles Postal Inspectors Office. An enclosed letter, pieced together from cut-out words taken from a newspaper, read: "Here is the Dahlia's belongings—letter to follow." The parcel included Short's birth certificate, her social security card, a bus terminal claim ticket and an address book with several pages removed. The following day, a postcard arrived that read:

> *Here it is. Turning in Wed. Jan 29, 10 A.M.*
> *Had my fun at police.*
> *Black Dahlia Avenger.*[8]

The letter writer never turned himself (or herself) in to the police. Instead, the rash of publicity spawned scores of false confessions. Thirty-three-year-old Daniel Vorhees claimed to have indulged in a torrid love affair with the deceased. His story quickly fell apart. Vorhees lied to earn a front-page story in the papers and his moment of fame. Twenty-nine-year-old army corporal Joseph Dumais, film bit player Max Handler, twenty-seven-year-old bellhop and former mortician's assistant Leslie Dillon, racketeer Benjamin "Bugsy" Siegel, nightclub owner Mark Hansen, Dr. Patrick S. Riley (a physician convicted of assaulting his secretary for sexual gratification) and a woman named Minnie Sepulveda joined a long list of supposed or confessed killers. All these leads and scores of others proved to be either fraudulent or quite improbable.

Hundreds of witnesses lined up to provide information, but all resulted in dead-end or false clues. Cab driver I.A. Jorgensen claimed to have picked up

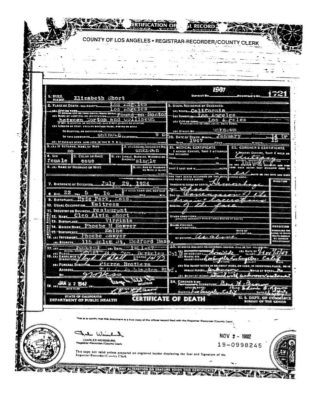

Elizabeth Short's death certificate. *Courtesy of* FBI Files.

Elizabeth outside the Rosslyn Hotel and taken her to a motel in Hollywood, a story which held a ring of truth, but led nowhere.

Author John Gilmore, in his book *Severed*, fingered six-foot-four-inch-tall petty criminal and alcoholic John Anderson Wilson, a sketchy guy with a pronounced limp. Wilson operated under a handful of aliases: Jack Smith, Arnold Smith, Grover Loving and Jack Anderson. Supposedly, detective John St. John prepared to arrest him, but Wilson died in a fire at the Holland Hotel on February 4, 1982, probably due to smoking in bed while drunk or stoned. Author Gilmore also named Wilson as a suspect in the unsolved murder of twenty-year-old Georgette Bauerdorf, a socialite found strangled in her bathtub after a brutal struggle with her killer.

The internet's *Black Dahlia Solution* implicated Ed Burns, one of Elizabeth's former boyfriends. Burns possessed University of Southern California Medical School training. In addition, he penned the following March 15, 1947 suicide note: "I have waited for the police to capture me for the Black Dahlia killing, but have not. I am too much of a coward to turn myself in, so this is the best way out for me."[9]

Mary Pacios's book *Childhood Shadows* indicted the temperamental actor, director and writer Orson Welles, whose sketches for the movie *The Lady from Shanghai* closely paralleled the victim's final pose. Pacios pointed to Welles's emotional instability, infidelities and huge ego as incriminating psychological reasons for the murder.

Janice Knowlton, in *Daddy Was the Black Dahlia Killer*, accused her father, George Knowlton, of being the murderer. Janice claimed that as a ten-year-old, she had witnessed Knowlton strike Elizabeth Short with a claw hammer in their garage and bisect her body in the sink. Janice charged her father with molesting her as a child, causing her to suffer from depression throughout most of her life. Janice died by suicide on March 5, 2004, at the age of sixty-seven from a drug overdose. George Knowlton died in 1962 in an automobile accident.

Los Angeles Times copywriter Larry Harnish pegged the culprit as Dr. Walter Bayley, a onetime chief of staff at the Los Angeles Hospital. His ex-wife lived one block south of where the body had been discovered. His office stood in walking distance to the Biltmore. He possessed the necessary medical knowledge to perform the surgery, and he knew Elizabeth Short. Dr. Bayley's adopted daughter, Barbara Lingren, had witnessed the marriage of Elizabeth's sister Virginia to Adrian West. Supposedly, Dr. Bayley suffered from early-onset dementia, which scarred his personality. Bayley died on January 4, 1968, at the age of sixty-seven. The list of suspects seemed endless.

Detective lieutenant Frank Jamison added Dr. George Hodel's name to a culled-down list of six plausible suspects. A string of evidence convinced Hodel's son, detective Steve Hodel, author of *Black Dahlia Avenger*, that his father had murdered Elizabeth Short. Mark Nelson and Sarah Hudson Bayliss, coauthors of *Exquisite Corpse*, concurred with Steve Hodel. Their thesis tied the doctor's motivation for murder to his attachment to surrealistic art and his worship of "eroticism, violence and irrationality."

Dr. Hodel was born October 10, 1907, in Los Angeles. Supposedly, his IQ of 186 surpassed that of genius Albert Einstein. A musical prodigy, he soloed on the piano at the Shrine Auditorium as a preteen. Academically gifted, he graduated from Pasadena High School at the age of fifteen and matriculated into the prestigious California Institute of Technology (or Cal Tech).

Hodel proved to be sexually, as well as mentally, precocious. He impregnated a professor's wife, breaking up her marriage and leading to his dismissal from college. The teen offered to marry the woman, but the older woman laughed off her younger lover's proposal as absurd.

In 1925, Hodel founded the art and literature magazine *Fantasia*, devoted to "bizarre beauty in the arts," prior to returning to college and graduating from Berkeley's premed program. In 1936, he received a medical degree from the University of California San Francisco Medical School.

Following a promotion to head up the Social Hygiene Bureau and serve as the top venereal disease officer for Los Angeles County, Hodel hobnobbed with the city's movers and shakers, including those in the art movement. His close friends included photographer Man Ray; Fred Sexton, the sculptor of the Maltese falcon used in the movie of the same name; and cinema icon John Huston, whose first wife, Dorothy Harvey, became Hodel's second wife. George Hodel presented an imposing personality. When he entered a room, the doctor commanded and received attention.

Hodel and Dorothy appeared to have an open marriage. His initial experiments in sadomasochism, partying, group sex and carnal deviations quickly matured into deep-seated urges, which he shared with his surrealist and artistic companions. To cite writer and poet André Breton: "Surrealism, like drugs, created a certain state of need and can push a man to frightful revolts."

In October 1949, Tamar, Hodel's fourteen-year-old daughter by his first wife, a model named Dorothy Anthony, alleged that her father had sexually abused her. The offense supposedly occurred at the Hodel family's Lloyd Wright–designed Franklin Avenue house during one of the doctor's lewd get-togethers.

Tamar claimed that her father had impregnated her and forced her to get an abortion. Police arrested a Beverly Hills doctor and his assistant the prior month on suspicion of performing that abortion on her.

The Hodel case went to trial, but on December 24, 1949, the jury exonerated the physician based on "insufficient evidence." Barbara Sherman, who previously had affirmed Tamar's story, recanted and refused to testify. To the dismay of many, the authorities not only acquitted the defendant but also remanded Tamar to juvenile detention. Tamar considered her Svengali father capable of all avenues of perjury, crime and immorality—including murder.

Hodel initially became a person of criminal interest to the police in the May 9, 1945 death of Ruth Spaulding, his secretary at the First Street Clinic. The doctor had ended their affair. Scorned and angry, Ruth threatened to retaliate by turning Hodel in to the authorities for illegally misdiagnosing illnesses, billing patients for unnecessary tests and providing unneeded prescriptions and treatments. She also claimed that he conducted unlawful abortions.

Lloyd Wright house built for John Sowden. Dr. George Hodel lived here from 1945 to 1950. Lloyd was Frank Lloyd Wright's son. *Courtesy of the Library of Congress.*

Spaulding died mysteriously from an overdose of barbiturates with Hodel in her presence. Dr. Hodel supposedly destroyed a number of papers before calling the police. The investigators had strong suspicions but failed to turn up hard evidence of foul play. Hodel avoided prosecution.

Dr. George Hodel. *Image from Wikimedia Commons.*

The police counted Hodel as a suspect early in the Black Dahlia investigation but again lacked proof of his involvement. On February 18, 1950, detectives installed a wiretap at the Franklin Avenue house. A recording documented his incriminating conversation with an unknown party: "Supposing I did kill the Black Dahlia, they couldn't prove it now. They can't talk to my secretary anymore because she's dead....They thought there was something fishy. Anyway, now they may have figured it out. Killed her. Maybe I did kill my secretary."[10]

A number of clues pointed in Dr. Hodel's direction. The police assumed the killer had transferred the body from the spot of the murder to South Norton Street on the empty cement bag that had been found beside the body. Detective Steve Hodel remembered his father doing cement work in the basement of his house around that time with similar bags.

Dr. Hodel maintained a close friendship with visual artist Man Ray, born Emmanuel Radnitzky, a believer, like Hodel, that "women exist at man's will and for man's pleasure."[11] Man Ray, a strange and talented artist, frequently photographed Hodel at his home and took nude pictures of his teenage daughter, Tamar.

In surrealistic art, women rarely appeared in pure human form. Rather, modernists substituted dolls, mannequins or bodies bisected and trisected into parts.[12] Man Ray's photograph *The Minotaur* (subtitled *The Destroyer of Young Maidens*) pieced together a woman's parts to create the head of a bull. The killer's disturbing pose of Elizabeth Short's body replicated the deconstruction of the female body that artists like Salvador Dalí, Max Ernst, René Magritte, Marcel Duchamp and Man Ray presented in their works.

The mutilation of Elizabeth Short's mouth—her Glasgow smile— reminded the *Exquisite Corpse* authors of the lips on Man Ray's rayograph *The Lovers*. Hodel considered himself an artist, a surrealist and a postmodernist. Steve Hodel believed his father probably viewed the posed corpse of Elizabeth Short as his own artistic masterpiece, his "exquisite corpse."

Witness Lillian DeNorak, who had lived with Hodel, identified a photograph of Bette Short as one of the doctor's girlfriends for LAPD detective lieutenant Frank Jemison. Tamar stated that her stepmother,

Dorothy Hodel, recalled George being out partying one night around the time of the murder and telling her that the police could never prove he had done it.

While looking through his father's picture albums, Steve Hodel came across a photograph he thought might be that of Elizabeth Short. As the detective pieced together his father's unnatural sexual urges, the death of his secretary, his artistic flair for the perverted, the cement bag and his surgical skill, evidence piled up that his father had committed the crime.

Man Ray. *Courtesy of the Library of Congress.*

As detective lieutenant Frank Jemison accumulated proof of guilt prior to making an arrest, he reported: "We know who the Black Dahlia Killer was. He was a doctor."[13] In 1950, with the investigation closing in on Hodel, the suspect skipped off to Hawaii and then went on to the Philippines, where he remained until 1990. He ended his days in the San Francisco area, not far from the Oakland Cemetery, where Elizabeth Short lay buried. He would live as a free man until his death on May 16, 1999, at the age of ninety-one.

The Black Dahlia case fascinated the public long after her death. The one-hundred-minute, 1975 made-for-television movie titled *Who Is the Black Dahlia?* starred Lucie Arnaz as Elizabeth Short.

Take-Two Interactive released the highly popular point-and-click *Black Dahlia* computer game, which incorporates Elizabeth Short's murder, Nazis and eerie rituals, in 1998.

The Museum of Death in Hollywood hosted a Black Dahlia look-alike contest in 2000. Orchestral jazz musician and composer James Robert Belden released his Grammy-winning "Black Dahlia" musical suite in 2001. The album *Ritual* by the group the Black Dahlia Murder reached the number thirty-one billboard spot in 2011.

Singer Marilyn Manson created watercolor paintings based on Elizabeth Short's image in 2002. Brian DePalma's movie *Black Dahlia*, starring Josh Hartnett and Scarlett Johansson, hit screens in 2006. More than a dozen books on the Black Dahlia have appeared since her death, and the crime has continued to tantalize mystery solvers for seventy-five years.

Elizabeth Short's grave. *Image from Wikimedia Commons.*

In July 2018, Sandi Nichols of Indianapolis, Indiana, sorted through her mother's effects. She discovered a "dying declaration letter" written by her grandfather W. Glenn Martin incriminating George Hodel (G.H.).

On October 26, 1949, Martin wrote a three-page letter identifying himself as a paid LAPD informant. The memorandum referred to "G.H." seventeen times as a personal acquaintance and listed him as the killer of Elizabeth Short.

Martin's letter also pointed to G.H. as the so-called Green-Twig Murderer. Authorities discovered the body of thirty-five-year-old hairstylist Louise Springer in her car on June 16, 1949, at Thirty-Ninth Street, a block from where Short's body had been discovered. Springer's executioner had beaten and strangled her before ramming a stick into her vagina. Martin specifically stated that law enforcement knew and protected G.H.[14]

The Black Dahlia murder of Elizabeth Short has remained closely associated to the Cecil after more than seven decades—further evidence of the hotel's magnetic attraction for the strange and the inexplicable. Other intrigues would follow.

4

SERIAL KILLERS IN SKID ROW

Several notorious serial killers have roamed the streets in and around Skid Row over the past seven decades. The dictionary defines a serial killer as a person who murders three or more people over a period of more than a month to achieve abnormal gratification. The slayer generally selects a stranger, often at random, with less emotion than that felt by a hungry shark homing in on its next meal. The FBI categorized perpetrators' motivations for murder in four basic categories:

1. thrill seeking.
2. financial gain.
3. anger.
4. the need for attention.

Criminal psychologists further subdivided serial killers into four nonexclusive types:

1. Visionary: A voice orders the violence.
2. Hedonist: He or she kills for sheer pleasure.
3. Mission-oriented: He or she kills to rid the world of a certain breed of person.
4. Power-oriented: He or she seeks to control the victim.

Two additional breakdowns include the psychotic versus the psychopathic killer and the organized versus the disorganized. A psychotic fails to differentiate right from wrong. The psychopath operates with the skill of a master manipulator who disregards laws, law enforcement and right or wrong. The organized killer carefully plans his or her actions, while the disorganized perpetrator works haphazardly.

FBI special agent Robert Ressler first used the term *serial killer* during a 1974 lecture to the Police Staff Academy in Hampshire, England. Ressler paraphrased German criminologist Ernst Gennat's words from a 1930 article about murderer Peter Kürten, the "Vampire of Düsseldorf." Gennat referred to Kürten as a *serienmorder*, which roughly translates to "serial murderer" in English.[15]

When asked how to avoid a serial killer, Richard Ramirez, the "Night Stalker," explained, "You can't." Once a serial killer sets his sights on a prey, like the proverbial deer caught in the headlights, that person most likely will die.

Serial killers represent a rare breed, estimated to be just 1 out of a population of 6.8 million. Men constitute the vast majority of serial killers. In the 1980s, the FBI approximated there was a total of only thirty-five serial killers in the entire country. Yet the Skid Row area of Los Angeles engendered far more serial killers than its supposed share. A group of serial murderers roamed the Los Angeles downtown area, but they may or may not have had any connection to the Cecil.

On November 15, 1944, during a routine cleaning, a maid in a seedy hotel on Fourth and Main Streets discovered the bloody, sliced-up body of prostitute Virginia Griffin sprawled across a bed. Killer Otto Stephen Wilson had lopped off her breasts and mutilated her body because he hated prostitutes.

After finishing the butchery, Wilson calmly walked down the street and took a seat at the Million Dollar Theater to watch actor Boris Karloff rise from the grave and take revenge on his enemies in the horror flick *The Walking Dead*. Jacked by his earlier kill and the movie's violence, the assassin propositioned thirty-eight-year-old prostitute Lillian Johnson at a bar, took her to a hotel room three blocks away and sliced her torso from throat to knees with a razor. He viewed killing hookers as his mission in life.

Witnesses described the perp to the police, activating a dragnet in the twenty-block area surrounding the two crime scenes. A patrolman spotted Wilson in a Fourth Street bar, lighting a cigarette from a matchbook taken from the hotel where Virginia Griffin had been killed. The suspect sat beside a brunette in a red dress. A trickle of blood oozed from an open cut on his hand. The police promptly arrested Wilson, ending his killing spree before he could add another prostitute to his list. Following a trial and conviction, Otto Stephen Wilson died in the gas chamber at San Quentin on September 20, 1946.

After applying for a day job and failing to get it, Denis Butler treated tall, skinny, unsuccessful coapplicant Steve Nash to a beer and a bite to eat at a local watering hole. As the two men left the bar and walked together, Nash acted increasingly irrationally. Once they reached the Third-Street Tunnel, Nash unleashed a four-inch blade from his pocket and without provocation stuck Butler in the stomach. The injured twenty-four-year-old victim fled to a nearby hotel with his attacker in pursuit. Nash caught up to Butler at the hotel lobby and kicked his fallen and bleeding victim in the shoulder, but he allowed him to live.

Twenty-three-year-old Robert Eche, twenty-seven-year-old Floyd Barnett and twenty-seven-year-old hairdresser William Berg proved less fortunate—all died from knife wounds. Nash had also beaten William Burns to death in San Francisco with a lead pipe.

In 1957, the police arrested the six-foot-three-inch-tall, bushy-haired, thirty-three-year-old, toothless Steve Nash, a San Quentin Penitentiary graduate, a week after he tried to beat another man to death in the downtown Third-Street Tunnel. Nash had paid the guy ten dollars to perform oral sex on him at a seedy hotel. When Nash pulled down his pants, the man ran, but Nash caught him and beat him mercilessly. Passing motorists broke up the fight and saved the victim's life.

Nash stabbed to death twelve-year-old Larry Rice beneath the Santa Monica Pier because he had never seen a kid die. He knifed the boy almost thirty times. All in all, Nash savagely murdered eleven victims, primarily in the Skid Row area over a two-year period for the thrill of the kill.

After Nash was sentenced to death row, a newsman asked him how he felt. The website Murderpedia recorded his answer:

> *"I'm the winner—like any champion should feel—king of the killers. Like any king should feel."*
>
> *"Do you think you're going to die like a man?"*
>
> *"What? I got plenty to die for. I don't have nothin' to live for."*

Nash died in the gas chamber at San Quentin on August 21, 1959.

Twenty-year-old eighth-grade dropout Vaughn Orrin Greenwood, "the Skid Row Slasher," knifed aging transient David Russell by the library steps on November 13, 1964. He killed Benjamin Hornberg in a hotel bathroom the following day. Greenwood fled the West Coast for Chicago area shortly after the murders but ended up with a five-and-a-half-year prison term in Illinois on an unrelated attempted murder charge.

Following his release, he returned to Skid Row, where he murdered seven homeless alcoholics in the fourteen-month period between December 1, 1974, and January 17, 1975: forty-six-year-old Charles Jackson, forty-seven-year-old Eskimo Moses Yakima, fifty-four-year-old Arthur Dahlstedt, forty-two-year-old David Perez, fifty-eight-year-old Casimir Strawinski, forty-six-year-old Robert Strannahan and, his final victim, forty-nine-year-old Samuel Suarez. The slasher cut the throats of his victims from ear to ear, carefully posing the bodies and leaving cups of blood on the ground and rings of sand around their heads. Some he killed on the streets, others in hotel rooms.

A police psychological profile pegged the killer as having a low IQ and being a homosexual Satanist—a visionary murderer. Two more deaths followed in the Hollywood area. On February 2, Greenwood invaded the Hollywood home of William Graham and attacked him with a hatchet. A guest intervened, and in the ensuing struggle, both men flew through a plate-glass window. Greenwood fled past the home of actor Burt Reynolds, where he inadvertently dropped a letter with his name on it. The police arrested him the following day for robbery and assault. On January 19, 1977, the courts sentenced Greenwood to life imprisonment at the Ironwood State Prison in Blythe, California.

The "Hillside Strangler," the killer of ten women, turned out to be two men, cousins Kenneth Alessio Bianchi and Angelo Buono Jr., both originally from Rochester, New York. Bianchi, born in 1950 to an alcoholic mother who was a sex worker, suffered from petit mal seizures as a child. His adoptive mother categorized him as lazy and an inveterate liar. As an adolescent, he continually wet his bed. The police suspected him in the Alphabet Killings of three young girls when he was barely out of his teens. In 1976, he moved to Los Angeles, where he teamed up with Buono, his older cousin. Buono had begun stealing cars at the age of fourteen and progressed to more violent offenses as he aged.

The duo terrorized the city, starting with the death of Yolanda Washington on October 17, 1977, and ending on February 17, 1978, with the death of Cindy Lee Hudspeth.

On December 14, 1977, the killers dumped seventeen-year-old sex worker Kimberly Diane Martin's nude body in an empty lot near city hall. The Hillside Strangler duo had called Martin's call girl agency. When the police checked out the apartment to which Diane had been dispatched, they discovered an empty building.

In January 1979, the Bellingham police arrested Bianchi for the rape and murder of two women he had lured to a home for a house sitting job. Faced with the death penalty, he turned on his partner, Buono, in exchange for leniency.

Apparently, the cousins killed for the mere enjoyment of it. Both men received life sentences. Buono died of a heart attack on September 21, 2002, at Calipatria State Prison at the age of sixty-seven. As of February 2022, Bianchi was continuing to serve his sentence at Washington State Prison in Walla Walla.

The "Skid Row Stabber" offed eleven homeless downtowners with a knife. The stabber killed fifty-year-old Jesse Martinez on October 23, 1978. Six days later, a second victim, thirty-two-year-old Jose Cortes, met his end. A day later, forty-six-year-old Bruce Emmett Drake fell to the knife. Other deaths followed in quick succession: sixty-five-year-old J.P. Henderson on November 4, thirty-nine-year-old David Martin Jones on November 9, fifty-seven-year-old Francisco Pérez Rodriguez on November 11, thirty-six-year-old Frank Reed and forty-nine-year-old Augustine Luna on November 12, thirty-four-year-old Native American Milford Fletcher on November 17 and forty-five-year-old Frank Garcia on November 23. Police found the corpses in alleys, bushes and along the streets around city hall.

In December 1978, police arrested twenty-nine-year-old Bobby Joe Maxwell, who called himself Luther, for deviant behavior against a homeless man who was sleeping on the street. Maxwell had moved to Los Angeles after his release from a Tennessee prison the previous year. The authorities confiscated the knife Maxwell was carrying and incarcerated him for several weeks. During his time in jail, the killings stopped.

Just three days after Maxwell's release, due to a lack of concrete evidence, the stabber murdered his last victim: twenty-six-year-old Luis Alvarez. The investigation heated up when three witnesses described the killer of David Martin Jones, who was found near city hall on November 9, 1978, as a Black man with a Puerto Rican accent who called himself Luther.

Incriminating graffiti on the wall of the toilet room at the Los Angeles Greyhound Bus Terminal read, "My name is Luther, and I kill them to save me from misery."[16] Detectives already considered Maxwell a person of interest, and his connection to the name Luther strengthened their case. A search of Maxwell's living quarters convinced the investigators of his satanic beliefs and probable use of the name Lucifer or Luther.

Detectives arrested Maxwell on suspicion of murder in April 1979. The stabbings abruptly ended. Maxwell's trial stalled over the next five years until 1984. Cellmate Sidney Storch, a snitch with a long criminal record, testified that the defendant had confessed to the murders. The similarity of Maxwell's knife to the one used by the killer and the witnesses to the Jones murder provided the jury with all the evidence they needed for the conviction of two homicides. The court sentenced Maxwell to life imprisonment without the possibility of parole.

Throughout his years in prison, Maxwell asserted his innocence. In 2010, lawyers presented evidence that the police had used undue pressure against the witnesses to force them to identify their client as the murderer. The attorneys also showed that Storch, who died in 1988, had provided false testimony in order to reduce his own sentence. Based on the new findings, the court granted Maxwell a new trial.

In 2017, Maxwell suffered a heart attack and ended up in a coma. In August 2018, the Los Angeles Prosecution Office dropped all charges and declared him not guilty. However, Maxwell died in April 2019 at the age of sixty-nine without regaining consciousness. Thus, the true identity of the Skid Row Stabber remains a question, but the culprit appeared to have been a mission-oriented or visionary killer, targeting alcoholic, vagrant males.

Serial killer Michael Player, also known as Marcus Nisby and the "Skid Row Slayer," murdered ten victims. He shot his marks execution style, with a single bullet to the head, generally targeting the homeless. As a minor-league felon, Player had served time for theft, armed robbery, carrying a concealed weapon and violating probation.

Player died on October 10, 1986, at the age of twenty-six from a self-inflicted gunshot wound at the St. Regis Motel on Wiltshire Boulevard. Ballistic tests on the .38 he used to kill himself revealed that he had employed the pistol in the deaths of four Skid Row vagrants. A search of this mission-oriented killer's personal effects tied him to six additional murders.

Louis Craine, the "Southside Slayer," a low-IQ thirty-two-year-old unemployed construction worker, strangled at least four women and possibly more. He targeted young Black women, dumping their bodies in alleys and empty buildings. With his own family's testimony stacked against him, Supreme Court Justice Janice Croft sentenced Craine to death for his crimes following a 1989 trial. However, he died in a prison hospital near San Rafael a few months later from AIDS-related complications.

Lonnie David Franklin Jr., the "Grim Sleeper," murdered no fewer than ten women, primarily Black sex workers, over a fourteen-year period between

1988 and 2002. The military had dishonorably discharged him for rape, and he later served time for theft. Arrested for murder in 2010, he received the death penalty in 2016 but died in his San Quentin cell at the age of sixty-seven on March 28, 2020, apparently of natural causes.

On December 31, 2020, serial killer Samuel Little, the "Choke-and-Stroke Killer," whose rap sheet contained more than seventy-five arrests, died of natural causes in California State Prison in Lancaster at the age of eighty. His mother, a teenage prostitute, abandoned him on the side of the road as a baby. His grandfather raised him. Little left home as a teenager to live like a nomad, stealing and robbing for his wants or needs. He spent ten years, off and on, in jail for miscellaneous charges of rape, assault and robbery.

Little murdered six nameless Black streetwalkers in Los Angeles in 1987, plus two confirmed victims: Carol Elford and Guadalupe Abodaca. He added Audrey Everett to his Los Angeles rolls in 1989, plus four unknowns between 1991 and 1993. A transient career criminal with artistic skill and a high IQ, he killed because he liked both lady's necks and killing. Murder excited him sexually. Once in custody, Little confessed to ninety-three murders, primarily those of prostitutes, by strangulation in fourteen states scattered throughout the country, making him one of the most prolific serial killers in America.

Skid Row, population: too many. *Image from Wikimedia Commons.*

Chester Dewayne Turner, the "Southside Slayer," a towering monster who tipped the scales at 260 pounds and a native of Warren, Arkansas, operated on the outskirts of Skid Row. He murdered at least fourteen women, mostly prostitutes, between 1987 and 1998, a few in the downtown area. He had been in and out of jail seven times for a combination of violent and nonviolent crimes prior to his capture. On April 30, 2007, the courts convicted the forty-four-year-old man of ten counts of murder and added four more on June 19, 2014.

Whether serial killers Otto Wilson, Steve Nash, the Skid Row Slasher, the Hillside Strangler, the Skid Row Stabber, the Skid Row Slayer, the Southside Slayer, the Grim Sleeper, the Choke-and-Stroke Killer, the Southside Slayer or any of the other unsolved downtown murders were connected directly to the Cecil remains a question. However, it stands as an undeniable fact that Skid Row and the area around the Cecil presented a very dangerous place, especially after dark. We also know with certainty that at least two serial killers lived in the hotel during their killing sprees.

THE NIGHT STALKER

Serial killer Ricardo (Richard) Leyva Muñoz Ramirez, also known as the "Night Stalker," entered the world on leap day, February 29, 1960, in El Paso, Texas, the youngest of five children. His father, Julián, a Mexican national and former Juarez policeman, ground out a living laying track for the Santa Fe Railroad in Texas. His mother, Mercedes, worked in Tony Lama's leather-tanning factory, a hazardous job site loaded with noxious chemicals. Even with their two incomes, money problems continually niggled at the Ramirez household.

The tanning fumes Mercedes inhaled, along with radiation from the nearby New Mexico nuclear test sites, generated a noxious environment that wreaked havoc on the health of the Ramirez children. When Mercedes delivered her first-born son, Ruben, he developed lumps across his back as large as ping pong balls. The doctors worried he might die, but his body healed, and the lumps disappeared. Their second son, Joseph, suffered a crippling leg infirmity, requiring multiple operations and creating a permanent limp—all possibly due to radiation poisoning. The cost of the children's medical care played havoc with Julian and Mercedes's strained finances. Their third son, Robert, and their daughter, Ruth, appeared healthy.

Mercedes's final pregnancy proved difficult. The tanning chemicals made her dizzy, and she required shots to avoid aborting. Nonetheless, baby Richard arrived without ill effects.

As a two-year-old, Richie, as the family called him, shimmied on top of a dresser to reach a radio. As he grabbed it, the furniture toppled on him, requiring a trip to the emergency room at the hospital for thirty stitches to suture the wound. Even more damaging, the toddler suffered a concussion. At the age of five, a swing smacked him in the head, leading to more stitches and a second concussion.

As Richie aged, his head injuries morphed into epileptic seizures, producing even higher medical costs for the family. He suffered petit mal episodes several times each month, but the doctors expected that the boy would grow out of the condition. The seizures, during which he stared vacantly into space, generally lasted only a minute or so, but head injuries often lead to aggressive behavior and a personality change. A group of criminal psychologists stipulated that 70 percent of the serial killers they examined had incurred a prior brain injury, much like Hillside Strangler, Kenneth Bianchi, who suffered seizures as a youth.

The oldest child, Ruben, hung out with a tough crowd as a teenager. He sniffed glue and filched odds and ends. Frustrated by his son's behavior and the unfair hand life had dealt him, Julián lashed out at his children with his fists when they strayed, just like his father and grandfather had done to him. When Ruben and his cousin Mike snatched a car for a joyride, Julián collected his boy at the police station, took him home and savagely beat him.

The police arrested Ruben a second time for breaking and entering, and Julián again manhandled him. While Mr. Ramirez bloodied his oldest, six-year-old Richie stood by helplessly watching. He cried and begged his father to stop. His brother's bruises clued Richie to avoid his father's violent streak.

At a very young age, Richie perfected the art of escape before the onset of a full-scale paternal eruption. When tempers rose, harsh words and physical punishment usually followed. Richie learned to slip away like a ghost to seek serenity in the nearby Cordova Cemetery, where he smoked reefer to calm his nerves.

Middle brother Robert followed closely in his oldest brother's footsteps, always in trouble. When bullies teased Joseph due to his limp, Ruben and Robert protected him with their fists.

School administrators assigned troublemakers Ruben and Robert to the slow-learning class at Bowie Junior High. Teacher Frank McMan, reputedly a pederast, privately tutored the boys at home while their parents worked. McMan also supposedly molested the older brothers. Robert remained unsure if McMan had abused his little brother. Richie remembered little about McMan, possibly burying any disagreeable memories.

The three older brothers left home to fend for themselves by the time Richie had reached the age of nine. Only he and his sister, Ruth, remained.

Robert dropped out of school in tenth grade and Ruben in eleventh. Joseph departed home after graduation from high school and moved in with Robert, then later with his girlfriend. Ruben eventually ended up in Los Angeles.

With his brothers out of the picture, twelve-year-old Richie hung out with his cousin Miguel (Mike), a combat-fatigued Vietnam Green Beret veteran with twenty known kills. Mike showed his little cousin Polaroids of tortured, sexually abused and mutilated Asian woman, with him holding a .45 revolver to their heads. One photograph showed a Vietnamese woman's severed head. Mike bragged of the rush he felt by having life or death power over these women. Rather than repulse Richie, the pictures excited him. He idolized his older cousin, who taught him how to play mini pool, score pot and shoot a .22. Mike instructed him in the art of invisibility, the ability to stalk one's prey and the use of military techniques to subdue one's opposition.

Mike also imparted his tough-guy, take-or-be-taken philosophy: life is unfair; sympathy is for saps; the riches of the world belong to those with the guts to grab them.

Mike's wife, Jessie, and Richie's parents disapproved of the older cousin chumming around on a constant basis with someone so much younger. On May 4, 1974, Jessie arrived home after shopping to find Richie and Mike in the living room, playing miniature pool.

"Mike, don't you think it's time for you to quit hanging around the house with a kid and go find a job?"

"Nag, nag, nag! Is that all you can do?"

When Jessie continued her harangue, Mike threatened: "If you don't shut up, I'm gonna take out my .38 and shoot you in the head."

"You don't have the nerve!" Jesse goaded.

"Oh, yeah!" Without further ado, Mike marched to the refrigerator, yanked out his pistol, aimed it at his wife and shot her in the face. Richie and Mike's two little boys watched wordlessly, stunned by the violence. Jesse dropped to the floor, blood pouring from the wound.

"Richie, you'd better get out of here fast, and don't say nothing to anybody."

A dazed Richie went home and remained silent about the killing, although the murder indelibly tattooed his psyche. His daily marijuana intake grew, and he stole from the neighborhood to fund his dope needs.

Seven months after the murder, a jury declared Mike innocent by reason of insanity. The judge remanded him to the Texas State Mental Hospital, where he spent four years under observation.

Jessie's murder, the impetus of two older brothers and a cousin as criminal role models and his father's explosive temper traumatized Richie. When an epileptic seizure forced his coach to cut him from the football squad, where he had started at quarterback, school lost meaning. He ignored his studies and grew long hair. His grades, at one time well above average, tumbled. His propensity to steal from other students and even teachers led his classmates to tag him with the pejorative name "Fingers."

This life-changing tsunami of negatives pushed Richie to spiral further down the wrong path.

During the summer, he hopped a bus to Los Angeles to spend time with Ruben in Watts. His oldest brother had developed a taste for heroin, burglarizing homes to satisfy his need. Los Angeles presented a cornucopia of riches for a professional burglar. The downtown Greyhound Bus Terminal served as the hub for Ruben and his protégé to interact with thieves and fences, exchanging goods and services for cash or drugs.

Thirteen-year-old Richie had broken into empty homes in El Paso, collecting souvenirs to celebrate his entry. He loved the power of invading a stranger's privacy. In Los Angeles, Ruben tutored him in advanced burglary, a master's degree of thievery. The plethora of prostitutes, the bevies of sexy valley girls and the vast selection of porno shops cultivated the impressionable youth's budding perversion.

Richie dropped out of Thomas Jefferson High School in the ninth grade to avoid wasting his time in class when opportunity beckoned elsewhere. He spent his free time hunting animals with a .22 rifle, sharpening the hunting skills his cousin Mike had taught him.

Unhappy with his home life, he moved in with his sister, Ruth, and her husband, Roberto, a peeping Tom. The teenager accompanied his brother-in-law on backyard patrols after dark, where the pair spied on neighborhood women in various stages of undress. Richie also picked up the preliminaries of Satanism and furthered his taste for drugs from Roberto.

Bad habits had sunk their teeth into Richie like a pit bull chomping on the neck of a rival dog invading its turf. His father, Julián, failed to provide the sympathy and support he craved. The cops had locked up his favorite cousin in Texas. School became meaningless. Even his mother's Catholicism offered little comfort. Life had disappointed him. He faced the world alone and needed to chart his own path. If God had not helped him, maybe Satan would.

Ramirez got a job at a Holiday Inn as a bag boy and maintenance assistant. After obtaining a passkey from a disgruntled worker, he robbed empty rooms and sleeping patrons. One night, around 1:00 a.m., he spotted an attractive woman undressing through a partially open window. With his teenage hormones racing, he slipped into the room and jumped her as she reentered the bedroom from the bathroom. He warned her not to scream.

When the victim's husband, a powerful Mexican, opened the door after picking up a snack in the lobby, he caught Ramirez on top of his wife. He swore at the attacker and pounded Ramirez, venom firing from both of his fists. The skinny kid proved no match for the husband, who blackened both of his eyes and knocked him unconscious.

Following an angry call to the front desk, the police handcuffed the teenager and delivered him to the hospital to clean up his wounds. Richie lied to his parents and said the woman had made a pass at him and that her jealous husband caught them. Luckily for Ramirez, the out-of-town couple opted to return home and not press charges. Without fanfare, the Holiday Inn fired Ramirez.

Once he was released from Texas State, Ramirez's cousin Mike continued to influence him, fueling his younger cousin's ride on the highway to Hell. Hallucinogens delivered new monsters and a love for Lucifer to Richie's convoluted brain.

In 1978, having abandoned his Catholic upbringing in exchange for a bond with Satan, Richie packed a knapsack of belongings and grabbed a bus bound for Los Angeles. He also toted a stash of grass to sell.

The downtown area's drug culture and the aura of depravity excited the youth. Ramirez explored. He strutted into Dave's Adult Bookstore by the Cecil. His eye caught a magazine on the rack about bondage. The explicit pictures of scantily clad, handcuffed women hammered at the sexual fantasies pulsing through his mind.

Los Angeles's vast array of drugs allowed Ramirez to expand his opiate usage. He mainstreamed cocaine and shot up PCP. The money from his sales of grass flew through his fingers and up his nose. To support his growing habit, he burglarized empty homes. When he was broke, he'd sleep in stolen cars. One night, he kidnapped and raped a lesbian with whom he had shared some PCP. The domination over his hostage lifted him to a higher plateau than the thrill of the rape or the euphoria from the dope had.

When Ramirez had cash in his pocket, he would hunt for a cheap room for eight to twelve dollars a night at one- and two-star hotels, like the Rosslyn, Ford, Frontier or, his go-to spot, the Cecil. The room clerks never asked for an ID or questioned him. He kept to himself on the Cecil's fourteenth floor—no one bothered him. He liked the solitude, the chance to binge on cocaine while blasting heavy metal music on his Walkman. He took to reading Anton Szandor LaVey's *The Satanic Bible*, a book he had picked up at the nearby Last Book Store. LaVey's philosophy made sense to his drug-addled mind, reenforcing his determination to follow the path of Satan.[17]

Indoctrinated with his belief in the omnipotence of Lucifer, Ramirez stole a car and drove to San Francisco to meet Anton LaVey personally. He took part in a satanic mass held around a nude woman's body. As he drank in the scene, the cool, reassuring hand of Satan touched his shoulder, promising him that the dark prince would always stand beside him. Returning to Los Angeles, he read another LaVey book, *The Satanic Rituals*. He called his mother to tell her of his conversion to Satanism. She cried and promised to go to church and pray for his soul.

While staying in a cheap room in Frisco's Tenderloin district, he committed what may have been his first murder—the killing of nine-year-old Mei Leung on April 10, 1984. He raped, beat and stabbed her to death before hanging her body from a pipe in the basement in celebration of his new life before returning to Los Angeles.

Mercedes sent Ruth to Los Angeles to try to save her son by begging him to return to El Paso. Richie refused to go back home, explaining that he then possessed a profession as a thief and that Satan protected him. Ruth recognized that her little Richie had been lost to her forever.

On June 28, 1984, hopped up on cocaine, a habit that cost him as much as $1,500 per week, with the lyrics from AC/DC's "Back in Black" pounding through his skull, he hopped into a stolen Toyota and headed toward Eagle Rock, a diverse community located in northeast Los Angeles. The twang of Angus Young's hot guitar electrified his thoughts:

> *Number one with a bullet, I'm a power pack.*
> *Yes, I'm in a bang with a gang.*
> *They've got to catch me if they want me to hang.*
> *'Cause I'm back on the track, and I'm beatin' the flack.*
> *Nobody's gonna get me on another rap.*
> *So, look at me now, I'm just making my play.*
> *Don't try to push your luck, just get out of way.*

A pink two-story apartment house drew Ramirez's attention. Death and destruction filled his brain. He removed a screen and jimmied open an unlocked window in apartment two, the home of seventy-nine-year-old Jenny Vincow. He gloated at the ease of entry, certain Satan guided his every

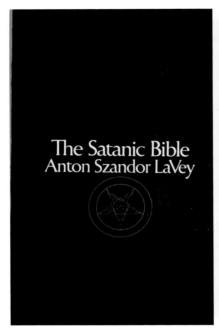

Left: The cover of *The Satanic Bible*, by Anton LaVey. *Author's collection.*

Right: Anton LaVey. *Author's collection.*

move. He possessed the power to dominate those within the building. He viewed weakness as an abomination. Might makes right.

As the intruder slithered toward the bedroom, just like cousin Mike had taught him, his blood heated. He flashed a penlight across the living room but recorded little of value—no jewelry, no cash, mostly inexpensive junk. Malevolence crossed his brow. He unfurled a six-inch hunting knife, entered the bedroom and plunged the blade into the sleeping senior citizen's chest. As the old woman cried out in pain, he covered her mouth with his free hand while slashing her throat and nearly decapitating the dying lady. As she gurgled on her own blood, the killer struck her in her torso three more times for good measure. The violence drove him to a sexual high.

Ramirez searched the apartment at leisure. In the kitchen, he calmly poured a glass of water and drank it, relishing the smell of Vincow's blood and a successful kill. After an hour of rummaging through the apartment, he took a portable radio and a few knickknacks and departed.

Ramirez considered running a stop sign on Weldon Avenue for the fun of it, but something stopped him. Just then, he spotted an LAPD cruiser.

Had he crashed the sign, he would have been cooked, caught with blood on his clothing in a stolen car. Yes, Satan had protected him, but he must remain vigilant.

The excitement of murder propelled Ramirez to an increased use of cocaine, and drugs cost money. His Colombian connection at the bus station, Roberto, wanted dollars, not promises. Always clad in black, usually in a Members Only jacket, Richie blended in with the darkness of the night, just like his cousin had taught him. He robbed homes, snatching anything of value he could find. Cash was best, but a VCR, radio, television or piece of jewelry contained value as well.

The drugs he received in exchange for his stolen goods stifled his appetite. Candy and soft drinks often served as his only nourishment for the day. His teeth paid the price, decaying, rotting and turning black from the sugary diet. He rarely washed, and he reeked like the smell of wet leather. Already thin, he took on a hungry look. A loner, he walked with Satan. He required no other friends.

Energized by narcotics, the days fused to weeks until one day, he recognized cocaine would make him careless. He cut down his intake of the hardest drugs, switched to pot and occasionally substituted or added a drink or two for effect.

On March 17, 1985, Saint Patrick's Day, Ramirez purchased a .22-caliber pistol from a skinny Mexican at the bus terminal. That night, clad in his customary black, a dark AC/DC baseball cap on his head with *Highway to Hell* ringing through his Sony Walkman, he stole a car from a gas station. He drove toward Monterey Park, some seven miles from the Cecil, where he followed a pretty little brunette to her condominium on Village Lane in Rosemead. As twenty-two-year-old Maria Hernandez pulled into her garage and stepped out of her car, he snuck up behind her. He aimed his "pistol at her head. As she turned to face the man behind her, she screamed, 'No, God, please don't.'"[18]

The swarthy intruder in black stood like an apparition a few feet away and fired without uttering a word. Maria raised her hands in a protective position, and the shot miraculously struck her fingers and the Weslock house key she carried, deflecting the bullet. She fell to the floor, playing dead with blood dripping from her wounded fingers. The shooter assumed the bullet had killed her, but during the ruckus, he dropped his AC/DC ball cap on the garage floor.

Ramirez bounded up the steps to the condo's kitchen. Maria's roommate, thirty-four-year-old Dayle Okazaki, wearing a Dodgers shirt, overheard the

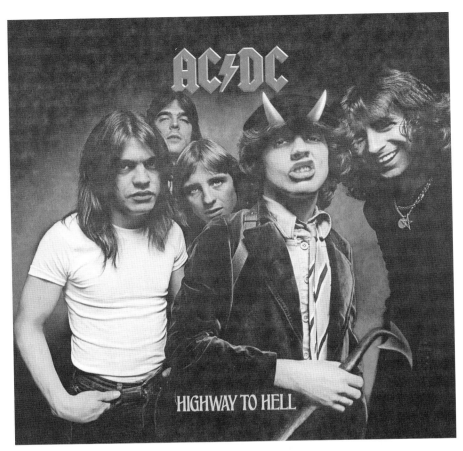

Highway to Hell, an AC/DC album. *Author's collection.*

gunshot and ducked behind a counter. When she lifted her head and peeked, thinking the intruder had left, a bullet struck her in the forehead, instantly killing her.

Ramirez trotted out the front door, where he ran into Maria, who had slipped out of the garage. Assuming he had already killed the girl and confused by her reappearance among the living, he fled to his car and escaped onto the San Bernardino Freeway.

Sexually charged by Dayle's shooting and the unbridled fear he had created, he searched for fresh prey. He spotted thirty-year-old Tsai-Liam "Veronica" Yu, an attractive Asian woman, in the vehicle in front of him. When Veronica noticed a man in a Toyota tailing her, she grew nervous. She pulled over to allow him to pass. Then, for some reason, she followed him. At a red light on Alhambra, he stopped his car, got out and approached the woman.

"Why are you following me?" she asked.

"I thought I knew you," he answered.

"Liar," she accused. "I'm calling the police." The woman's disrespect infuriated him.

Ramirez took note of the locked driver's door. With catlike agility, he pounced on the unlocked passenger door and yanked it open.

"What do you want?" Veronica cried out fearfully.

The man pulled out his .22 and fired into her side. She jumped from the car and ran. A second bullet struck her in the back. She fell on the street, bleeding.

"Help!" she cried. "Help me, please!"

"Bitch!" Ramirez answered, peeling off in his car.[19]

A man sitting in a nearby vehicle called for medical assistance, but Veronica died while en route to the Garfield Hospital.

Thirty-four-year-old, six-foot-four-inch-tall, 240-pound Gil Carrillo, the youngest detective in the sheriff's homicide division, caught the Hernandez-Okazaki shooting case. "Pumpkin" Hernandez, Maria's mother, had been a neighbor of his, making the case personal. Carrillo had worked his way up from gang life to become a member of the military; he then went to college and into the law enforcement ranks. His superiors considered him a very good cop.

Why would some guy in black shoot two nice ladies? Carrillo asked. He assumed the Yu and Okazaki murders must be related. Autopsies demonstrated that the .22 shells from both killings likely came from the same pistol. Carrillo contacted forty-six-year-old, six-foot-two-inch-tall LAPD sergeant Frank Salerno, a high-profile veteran officer who had run the Hillside Strangler task force. The two made a potent team.

With multiple murders under his belt, Ramirez knew he had pleased Lucifer. The more violent the assault, the more the dark master appreciated his minion's actions. He intended to continue.

On March 27, 1985, Ramirez again went on the prowl. He remembered a house he had robbed the previous year. He drove a stolen Toyota to the upscale community of Whittier, eighteen miles south of downtown. He rolled to a stop outside the Strong Avenue home of sixty-four-year-old retired CPA Vincent and his forty-four-year-old attorney wife, Maxine Zazzara. At 2:00 a.m., the couple slept quietly, unaware of the killer about to interrupt their repose.

Ramirez deftly removed a screen with his gloved hand and pried open a window. To muffle his steps, he removed his shoes and entered the den, his .22 drawn. Vincent slept on the couch with the television playing. The intruder fired a single shot through his victim's skull. With blood gushing from the wound, Vincent attempted to rise but dropped helplessly on the carpet into a heap.

Maxine sat up in bed at the crack of the gunshot. With lightning speed, Ramirez entered the bedroom and slapped her across the face before she had a chance to react. When she started to scream, he covered her mouth with his hand.

"Shut up, bitch! And don't look at me! Where's the money? Where's the jewelry?" Ramirez snarled.[20]

The intruder grabbed Maxine's hands and tied them behind her back with one of her husband's ties. He gagged her and yanked the phone cords from the wall. While Ramirez hunted for goods, the prisoner twisted free and reached under the bed for her husband's shotgun. The killer realized the odds had changed. He faced an armed and angry woman. She was going to live. He was going to die. He went for his gun, but Maxine pulled the trigger first. *Click.* Vincent had unloaded the weapon. Her mouth dropped. She knew she would die.

The killer fired three times. "You tried to kill me, but Satan would not let you," he screamed. He beat and kicked Maxine's corpse. Making his way to the kitchen, he picked up a ten-inch carving knife to cut out her heart. Instead, he notched an inverted cross over her chest and gouged out her eyes. Picking up a nearby jewelry box, he dropped the eyes inside—a piece of her soul as a gift for Satan.

The woman's blood covered his pants and shoes. He tried to have sex with the corpse, but the near brush with death had unnerved him. He couldn't do it. However, he discovered a trove of riches—another shotgun, watches, rings, a VCR and sundries—all of which he stuffed into a pillowcase. Like Santa Claus on Christmas Eve, he tossed the bag over his right shoulder and paraded to his car, rich with a retail value of nearly $40,000. In his left hand, he carried his precious box of eyes.

As Ramirez drove on the freeway with the box beside him, he vowed, "No one's gonna get the drop on me ever again." He slipped into his room at the Cecil unnoticed. That was the thing about the hotel—nobody ever noticed a thing, and witnesses wouldn't squeal to the cops even if they did see something. He cleaned his body and clothing of the telltale blood droppings.

With a handful of the stash in his possession, Ramirez left the hotel for the home of a pug-nosed fence he had met at the bus station. His connection ignored the bloodstains on the goods. With a portion of the cash from the haul, Ramirez picked up a prostitute to allow him to play with her feet, a favorite turn-on of his. He then dumped the hot Toyota in Hollywood and took a bus back to the Cecil around 6:00 a.m.

He lay down on his bed, lit up a joint and played Billy Idol's "Eyes Without a Face" on his Walkman:

> *I'm on a bus on a psychedelic trip,*
> *Reading murder books, tryna stay hip.*
> *Say your prayers,*
> *Say your prayers.*
> Les yeux sans visage.
> *Eyes without a face,*
> *Such a waste.*
> *Your eyes without a face.*

Ramirez opened the box beside his bed and smirked at the joke, his own eyes without a face.

The police investigators discovered footprints by the window of the Zazzara house. The .22 slugs taken from the couple had been misshapen, but the autopsy suggested the possibility of them coming from the same weapon as that employed in the Yu and Okazaki killings. Carrillo held a strong hunch that the same person had committed all three crimes. He and Salerno agreed: "We have a serial killer on our hands."

On May 14, 1985, Richard Ramirez popped out of bed. His fourteenth-floor room stank of sweat and marijuana. As always, he dressed in black and walked through the lobby of the Cecil for coffee and a snack at Margarita's Place, a half block away on Seventh Street. After a late breakfast, he sauntered into Ye Hi Pool Hall, flush with cash from the Zazzara gig. Unable to dig up a game, he settled on the Cameo Theater, which showed porno movies all day. He preferred flicks with violence and killings, like *Nightmare on Elm Street*, featuring Freddy Krueger, but pornos also excited him.

As he left the Cameo, he turned up the volume of his Walkman to allow a heavy-metal beat pulsate through his chest. He imagined being more famous than Jack the Ripper. The lyrics of AC/DC's "Night Prowler" goaded him to action:

I'm your night prowler, asleep in the day,
Night prowler, get out of my way.
Yea, I'm the night prowler, watch out tonight.
Yes, I'm the night prowler when you turn out the light.

The music carried Ramirez into an empty Toyota, using his passkey. A stolen police scanner would alert him to potential danger. He anticipated a night of excitement.

He motored to Monterey Park, a town jam-packed with good pickings. He parked on Trumbower Avenue. As a light sprinkle of rain sprayed his face, he played a little game. "Eeny, meeny, money, moe, I choose," and he opted for the residence of sixty-six-year-old Japanese American Bill Doi, a recently retired sales manager of the Santa Fe Trucking Company, and his invalid wife, Lillian. Like a ravenous fox on the prowl for a tasty chicken, he removed a screen and slipped through the bathroom window.

When he entered Bill Doi's bedroom, the click from the chamber of his gun alerted the drowsy former GI, who reached for the loaded .9-millimeter P.K. Walther on his nightstand. Ramirez proved quicker and shot Doi in the head with his .22 automatic, a weapon he had just purchased. Blood oozed from Doi's mouth. The intruder punched and kicked the seriously wounded resident into unconsciousness.

Ramirez flew into Mrs. Doi's bedroom. A stroke had incapacitated the fifty-six-year-old woman. He slapped her across the jaw and warned her to keep her mouth shut if she wanted to live. After binding her with the thumb cuffs he carried, Ramirez scurried throughout the house, retrieving a cache of jewelry, cash and valuables.

Bill awakened, moaning, and Ramirez knocked him unconscious again. The intruder filled two pillowcases with electronics and jewelry and slipped out of the house. Bill Doi somehow managed to dial 911 to plead for help before passing out again. The dispatcher sent an ambulance, but Bill died on the way to the hospital. With difficulty, Lillian described her attacker as a tall man with bad teeth who dressed in black. The local police failed to reveal two important clues to Carrillo or Salerno: the use of thumb cuffs and the presence of footprints outside the window.

Ramirez recognized the importance of learning from each crime. The papers reported that Doi had telephoned for help. In future adventures, he intended to dismantle the phone lines. Carrillo figured that the killer followed his own exploits in the news and tried to keep all details of the investigation out of the papers.

On May 29, Ramirez drove to Monrovia, twenty-one miles northeast of Los Angeles. He selected a nondescript beige house surrounded by a white picket fence, the residence of eighty-three-year-old Mabel Bell and her invalid sister, eighty-one-year-old Florence "Nettie" Lang. The devil worshiper arrived in a gray Mercedes he had snatched from the parking lot at the Velvet Turtle Restaurant. Entering through an unlocked front door with gloved hands to mask his fingerprints, Ramirez slipped into the kitchen to locate a knife, but instead, he grabbed a hammer. He tiptoed into Nettie's bedroom and struck the sleeping woman repeatedly on the skull with the weapon. He moved to Mabel's bedroom and cracked her in the head. She awoke with a scream.

Ramirez ordered, "Shut up, or I'll kill you! Where's the money? Where's the jewelry?"

"I have no money! Get out of my house! Who are you?" a confused and injured Mabel mumbled through her tears.[21]

The thief struck her again with his fist. He yanked the cord from the victim's General Electric clock, frayed one end and shocked the passed-out senior citizen. Ramirez left the unconscious Mabel and scoured each room of the house for valuables to hock.

Sexually stimulated by the thrill of the violence, he returned to Nettie, tore off her nightgown and raped the unconscious woman. He picked up a stick of lipstick in Mabel's room and drew a pentagram on her left thigh and another on the wall above her. He sketched the circle and five-pointed star, the sign of Satan, on Nettie's wall as well.

Finished with his work, he adjourned to the kitchen, where he calmly snacked on a banana and tossed down a can of Mountain Dew. He flipped a bloody pillowcase holding the night's take over his shoulder and ambled through the front door without a hint of remorse.

The next night, Ramirez pilfered a Mercedes and roamed the streets of Burbank, the home of Walt Disney and Warner Brothers Studios. He picked a beige stucco house with a bay window. The owner had locked the doors and windows. Always on the alert, Ramirez discovered a doggy door. Like a snake, he wormed his slim body inside the house. He drew his .22 and, employing a penlight, slipped into the bedroom of forty-two-year-old nurse Carol Kyle. Shining the beam into her eyes, he ordered her to wake up and not scream. "Who else is here?" Ramirez demanded. Carol told him her eleven-year-old son, Mark, slept in the adjoining bedroom.

The intruder grabbed the boy and cuffed mother and son together, ordering both not to look at him. He demanded her jewelry and money and warned her not to do anything unless told to do so.

Ramirez separated the boy from his mother and locked him in a closet. Returning to the bedroom, he tore off Carol's nightgown and raped her. She refused to fight, recognizing opposition might lead to her death and that of her son. He hurt her, and she begged him to stop. Her pain turned him on exponentially.

Once sexually satisfied, he grabbed a drink from the kitchen. When he returned to the bedroom, he complimented her as "not bad" for her age, and Carol thanked him.

"You're lucky I'm letting you live. I've killed a lot of people, you know." He laughed. "I'm going to bring your son in here."

"Please don't let him see me naked like this," she pleaded.[22]

Surprisingly, he untied her hands and allowed her to don another nightgown. After retying her wrists, obtaining instructions to the freeway and forcing her to hand over a few more items, he placed the key to the handcuffs on the mantel and left. Carol's screams brought a neighbor to free her.

Fear emanating from a victim elevated Ramirez's violent streak to a fiery pitch. He reveled when a prisoner shuddered and begged for mercy. Carrillo believed the perp had kidnapped and assaulted at least three little children between his robberies, burglaries and murders. There appeared to be no consistency in the age, sex or race of his victims. His size 11.5 footprint appeared at a construction site where he had raped a little girl. Ramirez later explained, "I was in alliance with the evil inherent in human nature."

In early June, Ramirez attacked again. In a stolen blue Toyota, courtesy of his passkey, he targeted the house of deputy sheriff John Rodriquez, just a few blocks away from the home of Gil Carrillo's mother. As he prepared to enter through a window he had pried open, the residents awoke. The commotion from the family induced the intruder to flee. Ramirez had made a mistake. He left an imprint of his size 11.5 Avia shoe beside the window.

Frustrated by his failure, Ramirez attempted to abduct a girl in Eagle Rock, but she screamed, broke loose and escaped. The would-be kidnapper fled the scene in his car. As he sped to get out of the area, he blew through a stop sign. Motorcycle cop John Stamos hit the siren, and Ramirez threw his pistol and an ounce of grass out the window before being pulled over to the side of the road. When asked for his license and registration, he claimed he had forgotten his wallet. The policeman said he would call in the information on the car, and if everything was okay, he would let him off with a ticket. Ramirez provided a phony name and address.

Stamos asked, "Hey, you're not that guy killing people in their homes?"

"No way, man. When are you going to catch that mother?"

"We'll get him."

"Hope so. I've got a wife." Ramirez lied.

When the officer returned to the motorcycle to call in the pertinent information, Ramirez bolted from the stolen car like a cheetah in full flight. He leaped over a fence and disappeared. He left a wallet with a dentist's card from a Dr. Peter Leung, a pentagram sketch and a black book with six phone numbers, but the cop failed to ask the tech experts to dust for fingerprints. Stamos's inaction permitted a valuable clue to evaporate.

Salerno and Carrillo contacted the Eagle Rock police to obtain fingerprints from officer Stamos, who happened to be off duty. The desk officer stonewalled the detectives to protect his turf. He refused to cooperate without the approval of a higher authority, citing "protocol."

Ramirez struck again on July 2. He cracked a lamp across the skull of sleeping seventy-five-year-old Arcadia resident Mary Louis Cannon to immobilize her. When she screamed, he choked and punched her, finishing her off with the ten-inch butcher knife he had taken from her kitchen.

Salerno and Carrillo drove to the crime scene, convinced the mysterious man in black had committed the Cannon murder. The detectives bagged the knife and cut a footprint out of the rug, recognizing it as the telltale size 11.5 Avia athletic shoe.

The police understood they were chasing a brutal and wily serial killer. In turn, Ramirez knew that he had to watch his step; he could not make mistakes. The papers printed composite sketches of him and warned the populace to lock their doors and windows to protect themselves against the "Valley Intruder."

The killer opted for a change of pace and location to throw off his pursuers, although he drove in his car of choice, a stolen Toyota. He selected the Bennett family's ranch-style house at the corner of Arno Drive and Lelino Street in San Gabriel. Finding the front door unlocked, he slipped inside like a shadow. He took stock of the entryway with his penlight, scooting into a bedroom of a sleeping girl. The sight of Whitney Bennett's helpless body worked him to a frenzy. He bent over her, cupped his hand across her mouth and struck her with the tire iron he brought, knocking her unconscious. Then, he hit her ten more times, intending to kill and rape her. He wrapped a telephone wire around her neck to strangle her, but as he squeezed, sparks shot from her body. The vision spooked him. Had Jesus or Lucifer intervened to stop him? He exited quickly through the window, vexed and confused by his inability to complete the kill.

Whitney Bennett required 478 stitches to close her wounds and multiple plastic surgeries to return her to near normalcy, but she survived. Ramirez ditched his stolen car and took a room for the night at the Hotel Lido on Yucca Street in Hollywood. However, he left a valuable clue in his wake at the Bennett house, another footprint from his size 11.5 Avia sneaker.

An investigation affirmed Avia manufactured a total of 1,354 pairs of that style of sneaker, but just 6 pairs found their way to the West Coast. Of the 6, only 1 was a size 11.5.

The detectives questioned victim Carol Kyle. She recalled the strong leathery smell of her intruder and identified the man who attacked her as being remarkably similar to a composite sketch the police showed her.

On July 7, Ramirez returned to Monterey Park to the tiny home of spunky sixty-one-year-old Joyce Lucille Nelson. The thrill of the kill stimulated him even more than the loot he stole. He seized Joyce by the hair and dragged her toward the bedroom. When she fought back, he beat her to death, leaving an imprint of his size 11.5 Avia shoe on her face. He ransacked the house at leisure, taking everything of value he could carry, before calmly and coolly escaping in his vehicle.

Sex and killing consumed Ramirez's mind. As a disciple of Satan, he intended to continue his rampage, vowing not to be caught alive. Later that night, he targeted the Hollywood Oak Drive home of sixty-three-year-old psychiatric nurse Sophie Dickman. He overpowered her, tied her hands and tried to rape her, but found himself unable to perform. He handcuffed her to the bed and grabbed all the valuables he could find. He ordered her to swear to Satan that she had handed over all the cash and jewelry in the house. She swore, knowing better than to anger a psychopath.

"Remember, I know where you live," Ramirez threatened as he left. He proceeded to the home of his favorite fence to cash in the goods from the Nelson and Dickman capers.[23]

The Eagle Rock police finally released the stolen blue Toyota and the wallet taken by officer Stamos to the sheriff's office. The sun had bleached out the car thief's fingerprints, but Carrillo and Salerno fixated on the dentist's card for patient Richard Mena, an obvious alias. The dentist, Dr. Peter Leung, remembered Mena or whatever his actual name was. Leung confirmed he had been in on July 3 and that his teeth had required extensive work that must have been painful. The police surveilled the office, hoping the patient would return.

On July 17, victim Mabel Bell died from her injuries without ever waking up from her coma. All of Southern California appeared on edge. Gil Carrillo slept with a revolver by his side. The Valley Intruder, the media's name for the killer, took pleasure in reading about his own exploits.

Ramirez's next foray occurred on July 20 in Glendale, ten miles north of the downtown. He attacked the bedroom of sixty-eight-year-old Seventh-day Adventist Max Kneiding, a service station owner, and his two-year-younger wife, Lela. With a machete in his hand, he flipped on the lights and shouted, "Rise and shine, mothers!" Max jumped to his feet, only to be met with a grazing blow across his neck. The intruder put the .22 gun to Max's head, but it jammed. As the couple, still in their bed, begged for mercy, he cleared the gun and fired it into the husband's head. He fired three bullets into the wife, killing her as well. Seizing household goods at will to hock, he filled a pillowcase and returned to his stolen car. His scanner reported shots fired in the area, and he hastened to his fence to convert the night's gains to cash.

The stolen goods trafficker noticed spots of blood on Ramirez. He sensed that his client might be the killer in the news, but he knew better than to make an issue. He vowed to end the relationship.

Later that same night, with the city asleep, Ramirez reached Sun Valley, a diverse community fourteen miles from downtown. He stopped the car on Charbonne Street and walked to the modest residence of Thai immigrants Chainarong and Somkid Khovananth, the parents of two young children.

With the finesse of a skilled assassin, he sneaked through their open sliding-glass backdoors and skidded into the den. The wife, Somkid, slept on the couch. She awakened at his entry, but he covered her mouth with one hand and pointed his .25 automatic at her head with his other, the pistol being an upgrade from his previous .22. He warned her not to make a sound or look at him. He tied her hands. Moving to the bedroom, he approached the sleeping husband, aimed his pistol and pulled the trigger. Chainarong died instantly. The intruder covered the fallen man's body with a blanket and returned to Somkid.

"Bitch, don't make a sound if you want to live," Ramirez threatened. He dragged Somkid back to the bedroom next to her dead husband. Had she struggled, he would have killed her.

Demanding everything of value, she cooperated. She led the intruder to her valuables. She swore to Satan that she had given him everything. Ramirez fed on his victim's fear. Her terror excited his lust. He dragged her back to the bedroom, where he forced himself on her.

He filled a suitcase with electronics, Krugerrand coins and a trove of jewelry, since Somkid's brother ran a jewelry store. After making her swear to Satan that she had given him everything of value, he left his victim on the floor, trussed up like a sacrificial lamb. She eventuality freed herself and begged a neighbor to phone the police.

With two black eyes, a concussion and multiple bruises, Somkid identified her attacker as a tall, dark man, maybe in his thirties and with bad teeth. She questioned why he had murdered her husband and had treated her so brutally. As a clue, Ramirez left another Avia footprint on the step for the detectives.

Reporters at the *Los Angeles Herald Examiner* met to brainstorm monikers for the marauding murderer. Rejecting the "Walk-in Killer" and the "Screen Door Intruder," the "Valley Intruder" morphed into the "Night Stalker," the name by which we now know Ramirez.

The Stalker awoke around 2:00 p.m. on August 6 at the Cecil for a late lunch at Margarita's. He sipped a coke and daydreamed about one day earning enough money to buy his own torture house. After lunch and a game or two of pool at Ye Hi, he fenced some jewelry from the Khovananth heist. He knew little of its actual value. Ramirez sometimes mistook costume jewelry for gold items and vice versa. He generally accepted the fence's initial offer. With a pocket full of dollars, he bragged about a few of his unsold trophies to a dealer at the bus terminal before handing him a C-note for a small bag of pot. He bought a paper and read admiringly of his escapades, then he caught a porno flick at the Cameo.

The Night Stalker's next assault occurred that night in Northridge, twenty-six miles north of downtown. He parked on Acre Street and selected the Petersen house. Chris stood well over six feet tall, and his wife, Virginia, also had some size to her. She was twenty-seven, and he was thirty-eight. They had a five-year-old daughter.

Ramirez first spotted Virginia. He shot her under the left eye with his .25-caliber pistol. Chris awoke and took a bullet to his right temple. "This must be that damned Night Stalker," Chris realized. Although wounded, Chris attacked the shooter, who ran. Both Petersens survived.

When later questioned, Virginia remembered him calling her a bitch. In a comment to the press, Salerno called the Stalker a coward. When Ramirez read the story, he grew livid. Each time he entered a strange home, he risked his life. He resented the insult. He was no coward.

On August 8, he cruised to Diamond Bar, a city twenty-seven miles east of downtown. He parked on Pinehill Lane, near a modest beige tract house. Heavily armed with an Uzi in his knapsack and handguns in his belt, sex, murder and money rushed through his brain. Forcing open the rear sliding-glass doors, he slipped inside, took note of his surroundings and entered a bedroom. Without hesitating, he pulled out a .25 pistol and fired a bullet into the head of sleeping thirty-five-year-old Pakistani American programmer Elyas Abowath.

The Night Stalker jumped on top of Sakina, Elyas's twenty-seven-year-old Burmese immigrant wife. He warned her, "Don't scream, bitch, or I'll kill you and your kids now."[24] He punched her to reinforce his power and blindfolded her with a shirt he found, ramming part of the cloth into her mouth as a gag. He struck her several more times, knocking her unconscious. This allowed him time to check out the house.

He returned to his prisoner in short order and slapped her until she awakened. "Tell me where you keep your jewelry or die!" She complied. When he dragged her by the neck into the bedroom, her three-year-old cried out for his mother. She begged her assailant to let her quiet him. When she swore on Satan that she wouldn't scream, he allowed her to calm the child while he watched.

Back in the bedroom, the Stalker raped the mother and might have killed her, but he looked out the window and spotted a passing police cruiser. As the car lights cast a shadow across the room, he grew edgy. He packed up a sack of goods, handcuffed Sakina to the bed and slipped out the door. Somehow, the injured mother sent her toddler son to a neighbor's house for help. When the police arrived, she described the killer as being six feet, one inch tall with stained and gapped front teeth.

Although the Night Stalker's publicity in the newspapers continued to please him, Ramirez worried that the police might be closing in on him. Frank Salerno had the reputation for getting his man, just like he did with the Hillside Strangler duo. A healthy reward being offered might tempt a snitch or two.

It was better to take a short exodus from Los Angeles, Ramirez reasoned. Even though Satan protected him, he needed to use his head. People at the bus terminal had begun to ask too many questions. He packed up his belongings from the Cecil and drove north in a stolen car to San Francisco, where he checked into the Bristol Hotel on Mason Street in the Tenderloin District. The location's proximity to porno shops, pool halls and his kind of people energized him—sort of like Skid Row and the Cecil.

In short order, Ramirez assaulted and robbed an older woman in Chinatown and burglarized a home in the Marina District, a preamble for more violence to follow.

On August 18, he motored to Eucalyptus, to the home of sixty-six-year-old, Wharton-educated, Chinese American accountant Peter Pan and his sixty-two-year-old bank teller wife, Barbara. He entered their quiet two-story stucco house, snuck into the bedroom and positioned the .25 pistol he carried onto Peter's right temple and fired. Blood spurted onto the sheets. He raped Barbara. When she resisted, he shot her as well. She should have done what he had told her to do.

Energized by the night's kills, he picked up Barbara's lipstick and boldly wrote "Jack the Knife" with a pentagram across the wall. With Satan's help, he intended to be greater than England's nineteenth-century Jack the Ripper. After loading a pillowcase with the Pans' belongings, he slipped out the door and into his car. Still keyed up, he picked up an ugly prostitute in the Tenderloin, paid her ten dollars and took her to his room at the Bristol for sex with her feet.

When Carrillo and Salerno learned of the double murder, they recognized the Night Stalker had relocated to the Bay Area. The pair flew to San Francisco to examine the crime scene. Word passed to the mayor Dianne Feinstein. During a press conference, Feinstein foolishly leaked the information about the killer's size 11.5 Avia shoes and the type of gun he used.

Wised up by Mayor Feinstein's slip of the tongue, the killer ditched his shoes, throwing them into the bay from the Golden Gate Bridge. The mayor had rubbed out an important lead. While Northern California lived in fear, Ramirez luxuriated in and around his hotel on a smorgasbord of pot, porno flicks and heavy metal music.

On Sunday, August 25, vacationed out and worried about nosy nellies at the hotel asking questions, Ramirez returned to Los Angeles in the stolen Mercedes. Rather than return to the Cecil, he rented a room in Chinatown. That Sunday, he drove a 1976 orange Toyota station wagon to Mission Viejo, some fifty-five miles to south of downtown, in search of action.

Bad luck struck Ramirez a critical blow. Thirteen-year-old James Romero III, working to repair a scooter, watched a car flit by on Chrisanta Drive. Some sixth sense perked up his internal alert button. The driver's fishy stare had provoked his suspicion.

Ramirez drove past and broke into the house of twenty-nine-year-old computer whiz Bill Carns and his twenty-seven-year-old fiancée, Carole. Without warning, the stalker shot Bill in the head, then twice more for good measure.

He announced to Carole: "I'm the Night Stalker."

"Oh, God, no!"

"Don't say 'God.' Say 'Satan.' Say you love Satan."

Carole obeyed, but the devil worshiper punched her in the face. He tied her up and drank in her fear, a magic potion that magnified his power. He raped her and forced her to reveal the location of all her cash and valuables. He threatened to kill her if she hid anything from him and made her swear on Satan that nothing remained. Before departing, he announced malevolently: "Tell them the Night Stalker was here."[25]

James Romero watched the car pass by again. This time, he wrote down a partial license plate. The stalker had wiped his fingerprints from the car, but he made a mistake. He left a smudge on the driver's-side mirror. When the boy learned of the Carns attack, he notified the police, providing most of plate number (482-RTS) and the make of the car (an orange Toyota). Things had begun to unravel for the stalker.

Petty thief and tough guy sixty-two-year-old Jesse Perez, a felon who once served time for killing a man in a knife fight, thought the guy he knew as "Rick" from the bus station might be the Night Stalker. His daughter worked for the sheriff's department. Jesse asked her to make a contact for him. On August 27, his daughter called the task force with a tip to get in touch with her father.

Perez supplied valuable information. Rick hung out at the bus depot and bragged about the greatness of Satan. Before providing additional facts, the informer wanted a guarantee that he would receive some of the $10,000 reward that was being offered for his help. The team assured him he would get paid. Then, and only then, Perez turned over the name of Felipe Solano, Rick's fence.

Detective Salerno discovered a store of stolen articles at Solano's house, many taken from the Stalker's victims. The fence cooperated to save his own skin. Rick, or possibly Ricardo or Richard, hung out at low-priced hotels, like the Cecil. The fence promised to call if Rick contacted him again.

The police recovered the stolen orange Toyota van in Chinatown, thanks to witness James Romero's alertness. The authorities lifted a partial fingerprint from the rearview mirror and sent it to the California Department of Justice in Sacramento for identification.

On a separate front, the San Francisco police made contact with a woman named Donna Meyers and her son-in-law Earl Gregg, who knew a professional thief from El Paso named Rick. He gave Donna several pieces of jewelry to hold. Earl grew suspicious of Rick after the Pan murders. He fit the killer's description to a tee—loved Satan, had needle marks on his arms, wore an AC/DC hat and a Members Only jacket, smoked pot and had chipped and discolored teeth. Earl also delivered a last name—Ramirez—but a very common one.

Detectives who had been pounding doors in San Francisco arrived at the Bristol. A resident described a man from room 315 who resembled the Pan killer. An inspection of the room revealed a pentagram Ramirez had drawn across the wall. The San Francisco police had closed in on the killer.

The results of the Sacramento analysis, using the latest Cal-ID computer, determined that the fingerprint taken from the stolen Toyota belonged to a specific Ramirez—Richard Muñoz Ramirez, a drifter, car thief and drug dealer.

Carrillo and Salerno then knew the Night Stalker's true identity and possessed his photograph. After discussion, the higher-ups released the information to the media against the advice of the detectives. In the morning, every paper in the area featured a picture and story on Ramirez. Although the Night Stalker remained unaware, the telescopic lens of the law had leveled its sights on him.

On Friday, August 30, 1985, Ramirez boarded a bus for Tucson to visit his brother Robert. He called from the bus station, but his sister-in-law, who did not like or trust Richie, told him Robert was out of the house. After another call and no invitation to come over, Richie returned by bus to Los Angeles, unaware that all of California was hunting him. The bus station had filled with undercover cops who were watching out for Ramirez in case he tried to skip town. None expected him to be returning to the city.

Once he was back downtown, Ramirez popped into Mike's Liquor Store on South Towne Avenue for a pastry and coffee, unaware that he had been outed. Two elderly Chicano women stared in his direction and mumbled, "El matador," in Spanish, translating to "the assassin" in English. This confused him until he saw a copy of *La Opinion* on the newspaper rack. His photograph stared back at him. Totally flustered, he ran out of the store and down the street. The store owner called the police as soon as he left, and a chase ensued.

Ramirez dumped his knapsack, ducked through a backyard and vaulted a fence heading across the Santa Ana Freeway. He entered a bus. When riders stared at him and pointed in his direction, he knew they recognized him. He hopped off at the next stop. A group of young boys tagged after him, whispering to one another. He warned them to get away from him.

The whirl of a helicopter a few blocks away alerted him that the police must be nearby. He needed to escape—and fast. His eyes caught a woman in a running car. He ran to the vehicle and told her his mother was dying,

"I must have your car." She refused. He grabbed her and tried to drag her from the driver's seat. Her boyfriend ordered Ramirez to get away from his girlfriend if he wanted to live. Richie took off with two toughs chasing him.

The Night Stalker leapfrogged a fence, ending up in the backyard of Luis Munoz, who was engaged in barbecuing hamburgers for his family. When Munoz asked what the stranger wanted and Ramirez provided an incoherent answer, Luis smacked him with an iron spatula on his head. Rather than fight back, Ramirez fled to neighbor Faustino Piñon's backyard, where the burly laborer worked on his daughter's Mustang with the motor running. The intruder jumped in the car and shoved it into gear. With hyper-alacrity, Munoz seized the wheel through an open window and yanked the keys from the ignition. The barely moving car ground to a halt against a wall. Ramirez fled from the stalled vehicle and vaulted a five-foot fence.

The perp desperately hunted for another avenue of escape. He spotted Angelina de la Torre inside her car. When he tried to force his way into the vehicle, she screamed. Her husband, Manuel, arrived with a metal bar in his hand. He pulled open the door and slammed Ramirez in the back of the skull. A battered Ramirez ran for his life with a posse of angry locals in pursuit, carrying bats and clubs. Screaming "el matador," the crowd closed in on its prey. Ramirez stuck out his tongue in defiance. Munoz struck. Ramirez dropped. More punches and kicks followed from the pursuing vigilante crowd. Within minutes, the police arrived, possibly saving the killer's life.

At the station, Ramirez glared at his captors with his dark eyes and pronounced: "You think I'm crazy, but you don't know Satan. Of course, I did it, so what? Give me your gun. I'll take care of myself."[26]

Hundreds of locals surrounded the station, where the Night Stalker had been booked, elated that he had been apprehended. When they took him to the same cell as the one that had once been inhabited by Hillside Strangler Kenneth Bianchi, Ramirez felt jazzed.

Carrillo and Salerno had yet to complete their job. They needed to button down the evidence for a secure conviction—that meant the recovery and cataloging of the necessary exhibits to enable prosecutor Phil Halpin to obtain a death penalty conviction. Multiple witnesses successfully identified Richard Ramirez, number two in the lineup, as the perpetrator. On September 28, 1985, the court

Richard Ramirez's mugshot. *Image from the LAPD's files.*

filed forty-five charges against the defendant based on assembled stolen personal possessions and positive physical identifications. At the October 24, 1985 preliminary hearing, an unrepentant Ramirez raised his right palm to display a drawing of a pentagram and mouthed, "Hail Satan," as he took his seat.

The March 3, 1986 formal arraignment that preceded the trial operated under the gavel of Judge James M. Nelson, a serious man with horn-rimmed glasses. Disagreement on which legal team would defend Ramirez led to a delay in the proceedings. After much discussion, Ramirez chose forty-two-year-old Arturo and thirty-one-year-old Daniel Hernandez, both unrelated and neither with capital crimes experience. Halpin paraded dozens of witnesses before the judge, generating a total of fifty-eight individual charges. With little to work with, Ramirez's attorneys stalled as a ploy to slow the process.

Ramirez initially contemplated suicide rather than face a trial. However, each day, a slew of supportive letters arrived from sex-hungry women, Satanists and crazies, all of which lifted his spirits. The Hernandez attorneys dragged their feet and fomented confusion to masquerade their lack of witnesses and exculpatory evidence. On May 21, Richard Ramirez appeared in court, sporting movie-star-dark sunglasses, to plead not guilty. A flock of female admirers fought for seats in the courtroom to catch a look at the defendant.

While Ramirez sat in the Los Angeles County Jail, the authorities incarcerated actor Sean Penn for slugging a photographer. Starstruck, Ramirez, in search of an autograph, wrote from a nearby cell: "Hey, Penn, stay tough and hit them again. Richard Ramirez 666."

Penn responded: "Richard, it's impossible to be incarcerated and not feel a certain kinship with your fellow inmates. Well, Richard, I've done the impossible, I feel no kinship with you. And I hope gas descends on you before sanity does....It would be a kinder way."[27]

California Superior Court judge Michael A. Tynan opened the actual trial with jury selection on July 21, 1988. The state had already spent the astronomical sum of $1,301,836 during pretrial. The Hernandez team hoped to stack the jury panel with Hispanics and minorities, who might display more sympathy to their client.

The selection process, like everything else in the procedures, proved slow and cumbersome, lasting until January 10, 1989, setting Ramirez on edge. He confessed to a sheriff's deputy that he wanted to sneak a gun into the courtroom and shoot the prosecutor. Attorney Phil Halpin, in response, stated that Ramirez had rewritten the book on serial killers.

On day one of the actual trial, curiosity seekers and Ramirez groupies filled every seat in the courtroom. The defendant marched to his seat, dressed in a charcoal-gray suit that admirer Doreen Lioy had purchased for him.

After the judge read the list of charges to the jury, Halpin provided his opening arguments, promising to link Richard Ramirez to the crimes via surviving witnesses, fingerprints, shoe prints, cartridges and other evidence.

The trial progressed slowly and with difficulty. Alternate juror Cynthia Haden displayed obvious sympathy for the defendant. On Valentine's Day, she baked "I Love You" cupcakes, sending one to Ramirez at the defense table. Admirer Doreen Lioy attended court daily to support her Richard.

The Hernandez team found itself overmatched, and the court brought in a seasoned trial lawyer, Ray Clark, to shore up the defense team. Nonetheless, problems continued. Juror Fernando Sendejas reported that he had attended school with the court-appointed public defender who had been replaced by Arturo and Daniel Hernandez. Although the potential for a conflict appeared infinitesimal, Ramirez demanded his excusal, which was his right. Alternate juror Haden replaced him. Another panel member required replacement after dozing off twice during the proceedings. Most unusual of all, a jealous boyfriend murdered juror Phyllis Singletary, leading to yet another switch in the makeup of the jury.

The prosecution called 139 witnesses and placed 537 exhibits into evidence during the trial. Following final arguments, jury deliberations began on September 28. On October 5, nearly four years after Ramirez's arrest, the jury issued a series of guilty verdicts in California's most expensive trial to date.

Judge Tynan pronounced the sentence: "Death is supported overwhelmingly by the weight of the evidence." Ramirez had attacked victims as young as nine years old and as old as eighty-three, including Asians, Hispanics, the healthy and the sick. The age, sex and ethnicity of his targets and the weapons he employed varied widely, but his use of savagery remained the sole constant in his attacks.

Ramirez, wearing dark sunglasses, asked to speak after the judge read the sentence. He rose and read from a paper in an angry and irrational voice: "You don't understand me. You are not capable. I am beyond your experience. I am beyond good and evil. I will be avenged. Lucifer dwells inside all of us. I don't know why I am even wasting my breath, but what the hell….I don't believe in the hypocritical, moralistic dogma of this so-called civilized society….You maggots make me sick. Hypocrites one and all. We are all expendable for a cause….Show no mercy!"

Judge Tynan cleared his throat and administered the death penalty nineteen times to defendant Richard Ramirez—"This penalty to be inflicted in the walls of the state prison of San Quentin."[28]

As Ramirez passed the journalists, he displayed a pentagram on the palm of his hand and announced: "Big deal. Death always went with the territory. See you in Disneyland."

That night, Gil went home to his family and cried with relief.

Carrillo and Salerno visited Ramirez several times before the local jail shipped him to San Quentin ten days after the conviction. Fingerprints and a confession made to a San Francisco officer linked him to other unsolved murders. The gift of a candy bar or two loosened the inmate's tongue, and he spat out details of his crimes.

The case had taken its toll on Frank Salerno. By the end of 1989, high blood pressure and arrhythmia led to an early retirement. He returned six months later but retired for good in 1993. More than three hundred attended his retirement party at Steven's Steak House in the town of Commerce, including Whitney Bennett, the beautiful young girl who was nearly killed by the Night Stalker. Plastic surgery had repaired any trace of her wounds. Frank's son Mike and Whitney hit it off and soon became engaged to marry, possibly the one good thing that came from the Night Stalker case.

Gil Carrillo ran for sheriff and lost but worked homicides in east Los Angeles and frequently spoke as an expert to police agencies throughout the country.

SAN QUENTIN STATE PRISON
RAMIREZ, R.
E-37101
CONDEMNED 06/15/07

Richard Ramirez, San Quentin Prison. *Courtesy of the California Department of Corrections and Rehabilitation.*

On October 3, 1996, Ramirez married Doreen Lioy in a fifteen-minute prison ceremony. He wore a platinum ring because Satanists don't wear gold. She believed in his innocence. Her family disagreed. After learning she planned to marry the Night Stalker, Doreen's twin sister, Denise, refused to speak to her.

In 1995, Ramirez plotted an escape while in court for a motion involving the Pan murders. The metal detector foiled his plan of using a hypodermic needle and a key to his handcuffs hidden in a vial in his rectum. He intended to bust loose, steal a car and escape.

The Night Stalker lived twenty-four years on death row. He drew creepy sketches of demon-like figures in his spare time. He and Doreen separated after she eventually recognized his true evil nature. He died from complications of B-cell lymphoma on June 17, 2013, at the age of fifty-three. Liver failure had changed his body color to an eerie green shade shortly before his demise.

The Cecil's undeniable connection with rapist, robber and serial killer Richard Ramirez solidified the "bad things happen here" notoriety of the hotel. The fourteenth floor, where he had stayed, served as a mecca for Satanists, cultists and believers in the occult who visited to drink in the horrors of the Night Stalker.

6

THE VIENNA WOODS KILLER

"He was polite, charming, very well groomed and dressed, and therefore, a darling of the girls," a juvenile parole officer said of teenager Jack Unterweger.[29] The Vienna Woods Killer matured into the world's first intercontinental serial murderer, spreading death through Austria, Czechoslovakia (today the Czech Republic) and the United States. The Cecil played a key role in his murderous ways.

Theresia Unterweger, a country barmaid, gave birth to a son, Johannn or Jack, on August 16, 1950, in Judenburg, a small town in the southwest corner of Austria, famous as the birthplace of the good and the bad, home of world-champion skier Renate Götschl and anti-Semite Nazi Walter Pfrimer. Theresia became pregnant after an affair in Trieste, Italy, with Jack Becker, an American GI from New Jersey.

Poor, pregnant, uneducated and unwed, Theresia drew a jail sentence for fraud, but the prison officials granted her a hardship release a few weeks prior to Jack's delivery.

The police jailed Theresia again in early 1953 for some petty crime, and the authorities shipped two-year-old Jack to his alcoholic grandfather in southwestern Austria's mountainous Carinthian region. The grandfather shaped his ward into what Jack called "a fraud's apprentice." The boy detested his time in Carinthia with a brutish *opa*, who taught him to cheat at card games and steal animals from neighboring farms. Jack wrote in chapter 7 of his biographical novel, *Purgatory:* "I sat on his lap, playing dumb. Later, I moved to my uncle's lap and betrayed his cards to Grandpa. I was the ace in his sleeve. His fists were my teacher, and I was a good student." Opa rewarded him for a successful night and beat him when the ploy failed.

Jack picked up his bad habits early in life. Grandpa taught him to sip schnapps while he still wore short pants. By the the time Jack was nine, his teachers considered him a school truant and a troublemaker. Thievery became second nature to him, and his grandfather's affinity for hookers fed his own love-hate relationship with women.

The boy yearned for his mother's love and attention. Theresia married another American named Donald Van Blarcom, a man Jack never met. His grandfather branded Jack's mother as "a tramp with no time for you."

Still morally and emotionally unformed, Jack fled the miserable Carinthian single-room cabin and his cantankerous grandfather to make his way to Salzburg, a midsized Austrian city of 150,000. He hunted for his mother. Instead, he found his aunt Anna, a kindly prostitute. At least, that is how Jack told the story in his writings. Anna treated him like her own son, but a john murdered her in 1967.

Unterweger got a job as part-time waiter. In his free time, he hung out with pimps and whores, perfecting his skills as a master manipulator. He traded in women and stole to make ends meet.

Jack's charisma attracted the ladies, but his violent streak terrified them. He brutalized streetwalkers. At the age of sixteen, he assaulted a prostitute with a metal truncheon, the first of the many crimes for which he served time. He spent the bulk of his years between 1966 and 1974 in jail for sixteen separate convictions, including burglary, assault and fraud.

In 1973, Inspector August Schenner investigated the murder of twenty-five-year-old Marica Horvath, whose body was found on the banks of Salzach Lake, north of Salzburg. Found naked from the waist down, her hands bound with a striped red tie, she died from drowning, following a torturous beating. Although the case went unsolved, Schenner refused to concede defeat.

Two years after the murder, Schenner learned of Jack Unterweger's arrest for raping a woman and assaulting her with a steel bar. With few leads, the Salzburg detective pegged him as a potential suspect in the Horvath murder.

Following one of his many releases from jail, Unterweger and his prostitute girlfriend Barbara Schultz plotted to rob her parents' home on December 11, 1974. Unable to break in, the duo forced a neighbor girl, eighteen-year-old Margret Schafer, into their car. Jack stole thirty marks from the girl's pocketbook and threatened her if she did not come up with more. A terrified Margret offered one hundred marks that she had at home.

After collecting the money, Jack and Barbara drove their captive down a country road to a secluded wooded area. Jack grabbed Margret from the vehicle and forced her into the forest. Once out of Barbara's sight, he ordered his prisoner to strip. She refused, setting off Unterweger's psychopath-power syndrome and fueling his anger. He seized her by the arm and dragged her deeper into the woods. When she continued to struggle and denied his demand for sex, he thwacked her with a metal truncheon he carried. When she fought back, he strangled her with her own bra and left her body face-up in a pile of leaves as a feast for the insects and animals.

Upon Jack's return to the car, Barbara asked after Margret's whereabouts. Jack answered, "There's no way she can betray us now."[30] Shortly after the murder, Jack, Barbara and a sixteen-year-old girl named Maria robbed a jeweler and fled to Basel, Switzerland. Jack came up with a bogus scheme to ransom Maria. When Jack showed up at the bank to pick up the payoff, Swiss police nabbed him.

Unterweger broke down and confessed to the murder. A psychiatrist labeled him "a sexually sadistic psychopath with narcissistic and histrionic tendencies, prone to fits of rage and anger. He is an incorrigible perpetrator."[31]

At his trial, the defendant testified that he saw the mother who had abandoned him as a baby standing in front of him as he snuffed out Margret's life. The court spurned his plea for clemency, sentencing him to life at Stein Prison.

Inspector Schenner continued to count Unterweger as the prime suspect in the unsolved Horvath murder case. He questioned the inmate at Stein on June 11, 1975, pursuing a confession. Unterweger stonewalled the detective, claiming to have been in Basel the day of the killing. Schenner felt certain that Jack had lied. When the inspector departed the prison following his interview, he viewed the prisoner's many deceptions as proof of his guilt.

Jack Unterweger entered Stein as a barely literate oaf, but with lots of free time, he read and studied to improve his language skills. In prison, after three half-hearted attempts to end his life by suicide, he acclimated to the routine, making the best of a difficult situation.

Journalist Sonja Eisenstein urged Unterweger to pursue an education. She helped him enroll in three correspondence courses on narrative writing. With his typical duality, he covered his torso with nasty prison tattoos while studying and editing the institution's paper, punishing his body while feeding his mind. He honed the lyrical quality of his writing, producing excellent short stories, plays and poems. As his skill as an author evolved, Jack developed a readership outside the penitentiary. He poured out the love he

Fegefeuer, by Jack
Unterweger. *Author's
collection.*

failed to receive as a boy into his children's stories
and filled his adult works with emotional fervor.

In 1982, the prestigious magazine *Manuscript*
(*Manuskripte*) published Unterweger's autobiography,
*Purgatory or The Trip to Prison: Report of a Guilty
Man* (*Fegefeuer* in German). The saga brought
him notice from Austria's literary community. A
second book, *Terminus Prison* (*Endstation Zuchthaus*),
earned Unterweger an award for writing. A film
adaptation of *Purgatory* delivered kudos from the
general population.

In the state of purgatory, a sinner seeks redemption
through suffering. Jack intended to convince a parole
board that prison had changed him and that he
should be released from his purgatory.

Unterweger's supporters included a who's who of European dignitaries.
Future Nobel Laureate novelists Elfriede Jelinek and Günter Grass, *Manuskripte*
editor Alfred Kolleritsch and sexual researcher Ernest Borneman attested to
his full rehabilitation. The governor considered Unterweger perfectly prepared
for freedom. At the closed parole hearing, psychiatrist Dr. Gerhard Kaiser
submitted a positive prognosis for his future outside of prison.

In his seminal book *Talking to Strangers*, author Malcolm Gladwell discussed
the ease with which experts can be fooled through a person's soft demeanor,
good manners and supposed repentance. Jack possessed the external veneer
to be highly convincing.

In 1949, petty criminal Jean Genet received a pardon after authors Jean
Cocteau and Jean-Paul Sartre and painter Pablo Picasso petitioned the
French president to set aside a potential life sentence. Once paroled, Jean
Genet remained a free man, writing dozens of important plays and novels,
even directing dramas and films, forever forgoing his past life of crime.

On the other hand, novelist Norman Mailer championed the release
in 1981 of killer Jack Henry Abbott, whose book *In the Beast of the Belly*
catalogued his years in prison. Just two months after his parole, Abbott
stabbed a waiter to death over a petty spat. Mailer excused his error by
stating, "Culture is worth a little risk." Would Jack Unterweger become a
Jean Genet or another Jack Abbott?[32]

The Sunday, May 23, 1990 edition of the *Kurier* newspaper reported the
release of literary lion Jack Unterweger, free at age forty after fifteen years in jail.
A photograph portrayed the articulate, five-foot-six-inch-tall stallion in front of

a café, resplendent in a double-breasted plaid suit and an open-collar white shirt. Sunglasses shaded his eyes. The gold lion's head ring on his finger, the bracelet on his wrist and the heavy gold chain dangling from his neck shouted, "Look at me." In other photo ops, Jack sported a white suit and a silk shirt to boast his savior faire. He swaggered with the step of an important man.

Jack's face resembled that of a cherubic young boy, but he possessed an aura of danger about him as well. His readings, television and radio talk show appearances made him the man of the moment in Vienna, the darling of the literary sophisticates and socialites. Schools studied *Purgatory* as the penultimate justification for rehabilitation. He spoke about his reformation on radio and television. Public news station ORF (the Austrian Broadcasting System) hired him as a reporter, where he commented on crime stories. Women flocked to him, drawn by his bad guy image and his "come hither" look. Magazines raved about the country's newest celebrity.

The ex-con pronounced his old life over. "Let's get on with the new." Writer Sonja Eisenstein, on recognizing his innate evilness, portrayed a darker picture of the recently released felon: "Jack Unterweger is a shark… an agent of destruction that threatens all society. No one is safe from him."[33] Intelligent but conniving, secretive yet seeking attention, Jack masked his true nature from the outside world.

Unterweger sported fancy clothes. He dressed to impress. He drove sexy cars, purchasing a sporty Mustang bearing the vanity license plate: "W Jack 1," the W standing for "Wien," the Austrian name for Vienna. Filmmaker Willi Hengstler, the director of *Fegefeuer*, confirmed Unterweger's narcissism. Jack didn't really love writers; Jack didn't care about literature written by others. "Jack only loved Jack."

Unfortunately, this monster in hiding's so-called new life proved to be an act, a sham, a coverup for killings. The slightest vexation would detonate his frustration into a full-scale explosion. When his play *Dungeon* received a negative review while he journeyed to the northwestern Austrian city of Dornbirn for a reading, the setback ate at him. He demanded payback for this insult. Bodies would pile up as retribution.

On September 15, 1990, hikers walking along the Vltava River in Prague stumbled across a naked female body. Thirty-year-old good-time girl Blanka Bočková lay on her back in a shockingly suggestive pose, a knotted stocking enveloping her throat. A gold ring remained on her finger; her clothing lay scattered around the remains. An autopsy showed the killer had beaten and stabbed her. Friends reported last seeing her with a nicely dressed forty-some-aged man in Wenceslas Square.

Prostitute Elfriede Schrempf disappeared on March 7, 1991, in Graz, Austria's second-largest city. Her parents received a call on their unlisted phone line, taunting them about their daughter's occupation. Police discovered Elfriede's skeletal remains on October 5 in an out-of-the-way wooded area.

Thirty-nine-year-old prostitute Brunhilde Masser disappeared on October 26 from Graz. The authorities chanced upon her partially nude, decomposing corpse in an out-of-the-way forest area in early January 1991. The killer had stabbed and strangled Brunhilde with her tights.

On December 5, thirty-one-year-old prostitute Heidemarie Hammerer went missing in Bregenz, a small western Austrian city with a population of slightly less than thirty thousand people. Her body turned up on New Year's Eve in the woods outside the city, discovered by hikers who found her partially clothed in a pile of leaves. A gag covered her mouth. Ligature marks marred her wrists. Her killer had tied and beaten her before strangling her with her tights. She displayed wounds to the buttocks, as if someone had stomped on her with sharp heels. The autopsy turned up a number of red fibers on her body that did not match the clothing she wore.

Unterweger appeared above suspicion regarding the rash of prostitute killings. The public's desire for his writings and speaking engagements remained at the highest level. The premiere of his state-funded play *Scream of Fear* about the AIDS epidemic opened in Vienna on February 17, 1991, enhancing his reputation as an Austrian literary lion.

On Monday, May 20, 1991, a sixty-two-year-old retired hiker discovered the corpse of twenty-five-year-old Sabine Moitzi in the Scots Woods. The man actually smelled her before laying eyes on the body. Once he was near a telephone, he called the police.

Vienna homicide chief of detectives Ernst Geiger examined the nearly nude woman lying face-down, fused into a bed of leaves. Wild animals had chewed flesh from the corpse's rotting buttocks. The stink of decay filled Geiger's airways, forcing him to gag. The strangler had used a stocking as a noose around Sabine's neck to suffocate her. The slipknot indicated he had taken his time to torture her in a slow and painful death. The contents of the victim's purse and articles of clothing lay scattered around her body.

The Wednesday, May 22, 1991 front-page headline of the *Kurier* alerted its readers to the potential that there was a serial killer on the loose: "Four prostitutes have gone missing without a trace from the Penzing neighborhood of Vienna. Now, there is grave concern for the lives of the three still missing. In the red-light district, the fear of death prevails." The public assumed twenty-three-year-old Silvia Zagler, thirty-two-year-old Regina Prem and twenty-five-year-old Karin Eroglu-Sladky had probably been murdered just like Sabine Moitzi.

Another body showed up on May 23. A woman seeking food for her pet guinea pig discovered Karin Eroglu-Sladky, who disappeared on May 7. Her corpse lay in a grove of spruce trees some ten miles outside Vienna. She had been a heavyset woman, and the killer probably forced her to walk some thirty feet from the road, probably late at night. There, he jammed a stocking down her throat as a gag, struck her repeatedly with a blunt weapon and strangled her with a ligature. A tree branch covered her head. The tip of a surgical glove sat close to the corpse.

The dead women came from the lower rung of streetwalkers. Yet prostitution in Vienna happened to be a relatively safe profession, even for the lowest echelons. Clients rarely harmed and almost never killed Austrian sex workers. The city promoted itself as a safe haven for tourists and residents alike, all eager to experience the music of Hayden, Beethoven and Mozart; the Belvedere and the Albertina Museums; tony hotels, such as the Bristol, the Grand and the Imperial; and, of course, Viennese wiener schnitzel, Sachertorte and strudel.

Many families dropped contact with their prostitute wives, daughters or sisters. Regina Prem proved to be an exception. Her husband, Rudolf, begged for information concerning his spouse, offering a reward of 10,000 shillings, or approximately $1,000, for information leading to his wife's safe return. He described her as a wonderful mother until she became addicted to sleeping pills.

Once she was caught up in the drug scene, thirty-three-year-old Regina worked the streets, but her husband loved her nonetheless. Rudolf Prem advised the police that someone had telephoned him and his son twice to taunt him about his wife's disappearance. The caller described the clothing she wore on the night of her disappearance and moralized that God had ordained her punishment as a sinner.

All Vienna nervously awaited news on the missing women. Prostitutes feared plying their wares with a serial killer on the loose. The police nicknamed the killer "Jack the Struggler," a play on Jack the Ripper and a misspelling of the English word "Strangler." The terrifying movie *Silence of the Lambs*, with Anthony Hopkins, played in the theaters. Unterweger called it a positively brilliant film.

Unterweger interviewed prostitutes for his ORF shows and newspaper articles. Along the way, he paid for sex from the women he questioned, several of whom he asked to wear handcuffs during sex. Most prostitutes consented. Unusual requests proved to be quite common to the women of the streets.

August Schenner, the dapper, highly suspicious, seventy-year-old retired Salzburg detective, phoned the homicide department in Vienna with a tip to check out Jack Unterweger as a suspect. Unfortunately, the detectives failed to pass the tip to chief of police Max Edelbacher for several days.

On June 3, freelance reporter Jack Unterweger of ORF wandered into police headquarters to interview the chief about the murders for an upcoming *Journal Panorama* radio show. The reporter advised Edelbacher that his aunt Anna had died in 1967 at the hands of one of her clients. The law officer confessed to the reporter that the police lacked a solid lead in the case. No one other than Rudolf Prem had even contacted his team with information.

Unterweger parlayed his interview into an article for the weekly newspaper *Falter* and for a June 5 radio show titled *Fear in the Red-Light District* (*Angst im Rotlicht Milieu*). To add a touch of humanity, he interviewed sex workers who expressed concern for their own safety and that of the other girls. Jack philosophized that society had failed to safeguard its most vulnerable women.

Although the ladies watched out for one another, protection against a murderer proved impossible. During the broadcast, the announcer informed the audience that prostitutes had been murdered or went missing in the Austrian cities of Graz and Bregenz as well, amplifying the country's growing hysteria.[34]

While listening to the program, Edelbacher mentioned to his wife that Unterweger had interviewed him for the radio show.

"Don't you know who he is?" she asked.

"No"

"Unterweger is that guy who got a life sentence for murdering a woman and who wrote a crazy book in prison. He was released last year."[35]

Unterweger suddenly became a person of interest to the Viennese police. Edelbacher assigned thirty-six-year-old University of Vienna graduate, attorney and law enforcement officer Dr. Ernest Geiger as the department's lead investigator.

Geiger possessed a keen mind and a law doctorate, but he had scant experience with homicides and none with serial killers. Vienna, a laid-back city with a population exceeding 1.5 million, reached a thirty-year-high annual rate of 50 homicides, a ratio of 1 per every 30,000 people. To place that statistic in perspective, in the same year, Los Angeles, a city of 3.5

million experienced 983 murders, a ratio of 1 per 3,560, which translated to an almost nine-times-greater number of fatalities. The appearance of the Vienna Woods Killer required an upgrade in Vienna's apprehension and investigation protocols. Geiger placed Unterweger under surveillance.

Although inspector Geiger possessed scant experience with serial killers, he questioned dozens of pimps and prostitutes, seeking leads, but he came up empty-handed. He lacked direct evidence tying Unterweger to the crimes, aside from Schenner's tip.

Unterweger returned to police headquarters on June 10. He informed Edelbacher that he planned to fly to Los Angeles for a story to reveal America's attitudes regarding prostitution. The reporter asked if the chief could suggest law enforcement contacts in the states. The chief could provide none, nor did he advise the reporter that he might be a suspect.

Unterweger arrived at the Vienna International Airport for his departure to the states, clad in a garish white cowboy coat stitched with a hibiscus flower design and snakeskin boots. He topped off his garb with a white ten-gallon hat for the flight to Los Angeles. The jewelry hanging from his neck and the lion head ring on his finger cemented his outlandish appearance. The sight of the undersized stranger in his Western garb pushed spectators to gawk and whisper to one another like they would at some circus freak show.

Jack relished the attention. Upon landing, he rented a car and drove directly to the Cecil. He knew its reputation as the house of Richard Ramirez and the home of the bizarre—the very reason why he had selected that hotel. The Cecil's location sat in the heart of prostitute city, on the edge of Skid Row, the perfect spot for his upcoming story and an ideal location to score a prostitute or two for fun.

The impressive entryway to the Cecil surprised him; it was far nicer than expected. He eyed the stained-glass ceiling, the bannister railings and the inlaid marble floors. He had expected a dump, but the hotel lobby possessed a pedigree—if a slightly tarnished one.

He sashayed to the front check-in desk. A friendly and cute receptionist, Carolina, looked like a lady he might like to have. She took in his crazy outfit and warned him to be careful in the neighborhood, which could be very rough after dark. Jack assured her he could take care of himself. He also planned to see more of Carolina, and she of him. His room on the fifteenth floor, although under-furnished and small, offered clear visibility of the street below him. He liked what he saw.

On Monday, June 24, Unterweger entered the downtown Parker Center Police Headquarters on Los Angeles Street and wangled his way into the

Top: Jack Unterweger. *Image from Wikimedia Commons.*

Bottom: The Cecil Hotel's reception area. *Courtesy of Alejandro Jofré, Creative Commons.*

ride-along-with-a-cop program. He allegedly held a job as a full-time journalist for an Austrian police journal, a stretch of his actual credentials as an ORF guest reporter. While riding in the patrol car, officer Steve Staples recalled that he asked few questions about prostitution but did comment about a couple of the more attractive law enforcement ladies he had met prior to the drive.

As planned, he interviewed prostitutes with a tape recorder the following day. In the evening, he invited a hooker to join him in his room for sex. The city provided everything his perverted mind had anticipated.

Somewhat starstruck, Jack purchased a home-of-the-stars map. He tried to interview Zsa Zsa Gabor and Cher at their homes, but protectors refused him admittance at both locations. He knocked on the door of filmmaker Robert Dornhelm, a fellow Austrian of Hungarian descent, to pitch his screenplay *Love to the Point of Madness* (*Liebe bis zum Wahnsinn*) for a potential American movie. The director displayed no interest. Rejection put Unterweger in a foul mood. That night, a prostitute would lose her life.

On July 2, toward the end of his American adventure, Unterweger marched to the front desk in a huff. He carped that someone had stolen an item from his room. He demanded that the receptionist allow him to check out at once. She agreed.

The cooperation at the front desk cooled his temper.

"Carolina, my crazy chicken, I shall let you know where I shall be staying," he told the receptionist with a wink. He moved to a Hollywood hotel.

Employing his magnetism and literary fame, Jack manipulated and seduced Carolina. Like a bee drawn to the pollen of a flower, women lined up for his bed. With his Los Angeles interviews complete, he made plans to return to Vienna. He invited the receptionist to visit him, and she agreed.

On July 11, 1991, a solar eclipse shaded the West Coast sky. Two men and their children made their way to a high point along Corral Canyon Road in Malibu to obtain an unobstructed view. The gruesome sight of a dead body stopped the hikers in their tracks. One adult witness stammered and swore on the phone during his call to the sheriff's department, overwhelmed by the sight of the corpse. He failed to communicate details and location coherently. His friend grabbed the phone from his hand and provided an accurate site description of the crime scene.

Deputy Sheriff Ronnie Lancaster learned of the death with an added concern. "Hope it's not a decomposition," he muttered with his slow Texan drawl. Lancaster hated rotting bodies. Arriving a few hours later, at 2:45 p.m. on a crispy, hot day, he encountered the carcass of a putrid, thick-set woman—just what he feared, a decomp.

The stink of death and decay assaulted his nostrils. The victim lay on her back, maggots crawling from her facial orifices, a sure sign she had died several days earlier, perhaps as long as a week. A knotted bra hung around her neck like a ravenous anaconda. The pockets of her jeans had been turned inside out. The recovery team collected one of her boots.

A fingerprint comparison with her rap sheet identified the homicide victim as prostitute Sherri Ann Long, also known as Peggy Booth. She generally worked the streets around Sunset Boulevard. Although she sought fame on the silver screen, her lack of cash and education drove her to the streets; a growing need for drugs kept her there.

Dr. Rabe of the coroner's office estimated the time of death at somewhere between four to seven days earlier. The killer had strangled her.

Long's homicide reminded the detectives of the recent June 19 killing of twenty-year-old hooker Shannon Exley. Her blond hair and clean-cut look made her a popular item with the produce district truckers along Seventh Avenue. The locals considered her a "strawberry," a young girl selling her body for drug money. Earlier that night, she had phoned her father and promised to reform herself. Unfortunately, the killer had snuffed out her life before she had the chance to change her ways.

Detective Fred Miller, a Vietnam veteran and a skilled LAPD detective known for arresting serial killer Louis Craine, the "Southside Slayer," perused the June 24 homicide teletype at the Parker Centre Police Headquarters. The parallels between the Long and Exley murders appeared too obvious to ignore. The skill of the garroter convinced the detective that the perpetrator had killed before and probably would do so again.

On June 28, a homeless man who was hunting for firewood along the Los Angeles River stumbled on the dead body of a girl in a Myers Street freight parking lot in Boyles Heights. The killer had dragged the body next to a large trailer at the base of a eucalyptus tree. Police identified the dead woman as thirty-three-year-old Irene Rodriguez. An addiction to heroin pushed her to turn tricks to support her habit.

Dr. Lynne Herold, an experienced medical examiner, nicknamed "the Boa" for her ability to wrap her hands around a case, had investigated nearly three thousand homicides during her career. She meticulously examined the similarities of the ligatures used to strangle all three prostitutes. Each bra displayed an incision in the same place and a complex knot. Like detective Miller, the similarities in the killings convinced her that one person had committed all three murders.

Deputy Lancaster and detective Miller knew coincidences rarely happened on the crime front. Three murders in just fifteen days convinced them a serial killer was on the loose, but the killings suddenly stopped—a most unusual situation.

Actually, Unterweger had left Los Angeles and had flown back to Austria. He enjoyed his time in the United States, but going home felt right. Upon his return, the app TikTok featured a short video of Jack's life story, as told in *Purgatory*. Carolina flew in from Los Angeles and joined him a few days later. This chameleon, with the ability to change personalities in a moment's notice, believed he remained in the clear. He had fooled the public. He thought he had fooled the police, but a small cadre of detectives stuck to the premise "once a killer always a killer."

Inspector Geiger's gut convinced him of Jack Unterweger's guilt. That knowledge gnawed at him. He analyzed the suspect's movements during the period when each of the seven European murders occurred. Poring over the gas receipts, credit cards, car rental contracts and restaurant bills that he could obtain, the detective constructed a pattern of evidence. He found that the writer had been in Graz when Brunhilde Masser died, and he was there again when Elfriede Schrempf disappeared.

On August 4, Austrian hikers identified the remains of Silvia Zagler three months after her disappearance. The body appeared virtually unrecognizable.

On August 16, Jack spoke to a woman at a café, who called him a liar. He threatened that if she did not keep her mouth shut, something might happen to her. She believed that Jack could be violent.

With a fist full of circumstantial evidence, Geiger questioned Unterweger to ferret out a confession on October 22, 1991. When the subject of gas receipts arose, Jack told Geiger he did not drive, as he had failed to obtain a license. That was a lie. Dozens of witnesses had seen Unterweger drive and recognized his vanity license plate. The suspect's alibis for key dates lacked the ring of truth. The detective knew the cardinal rule of interrogation: catch a suspect in a single lie, and you were dealing with a liar.

"Am I a suspect?" Unterweger asked.

"Yes," Geiger shot back in reply.

Unterweger promised to return with proof of an alibi for the death dates within two weeks.

A nineteen-year-old prostitute named Joanna from Graz came forward and advised the police that a photograph of Jack Unterweger in the newspaper resembled the man who was driving a car with a license plate that read, "Jack 1," who paid her to take off her clothes. As she lay on her belly, the client handcuffed her wrists behind her back and hurt her. She obeyed his orders, and the client eventually drove her back to Graz, but she believed him to be dangerous. The incident occurred in 1990, prior to the murders.

Jack quickly tired of the receptionist Carolina, and he told her to return to the United States. In short order, he found a new girl, Bianca Mrak. He met her in a Vienna nightclub a few weeks before her eighteenth birthday. When she looked his way, she patted the seat next to her as a signal for him to join her. In a typical male power play, he motioned for her to move beside him. She obeyed, and he literally charmed the pants off her.

Bianca moved in with him, and he proved to be a domineering control freak. He did not permit her to smoke. He demanded she wash his clothes and keep the rooms clean. He awoke at 6:00 a.m., just as he had done for fifteen years in prison.

Jack liked women supporting him. He encouraged Bianca to become a sex worker to bring in cash. She refused but took a job as a barkeep. When she caught her new boyfriend cheating on her, she threatened to leave. He apologized and proposed. She accepted.

The police continued to collect evidence and close in on Jack. Eventually, the detectives obtained enough to nab him.

The Saturday, February 14 issue of the Graz newspaper, *Klein's Zeitung*, notified the public and Unterweger that a warrant had been issued for his arrest. To escape his pursuers, the suspect skipped across the border to Switzerland.

Bianca recognized Jack's idiosyncrasies but believed in his innocence. He looked too sweet to do something so bad. How could a man with such carefully manicured hands kill?

She agreed to escape with him by car to France. In Paris, the couple ditched their BMW near the airport. The police located, confiscated and searched the car, finding a hair fragment, which they sent to the University of Bern lab for analysis. The DNA matched that of murdered Prague party girl Blanka Bočková and tied Unterweger directly to one of the victims.

Bianca maintained a teenage crush on actor Don Johnson, who played Detective Sonny Crockett on the American television show *Miami Vice*. She asked Jack to take her to Florida.

The couple caught a flight from Orly in Paris, landed in Canada and transferred to Miami. Once the duo reached Florida, reality crushed Bianca's dreams of money, excitement and the high life. Instead, she found herself in a seedy, cockroach-ridden hotel. Jack again asked her to sell her body for money. She refused but took a job she hated at Miami Gold as a go-go girl.

Unterweger phoned the Austrian media to complain about the police hounding him. "I am an innocent man. Why are you persecuting me?" He offered to return to Austria for questioning—but only if the police removed all warrants.

With Unterweger out of the country, Geiger and a SWAT team raided his apartment. Pictures of Jack with female Los Angeles police officers sat on a nightstand. The police confiscated handcuffs, mace and a knife—all illegal for a felon to own. The team seized Jack's diary, but he had torn out and destroyed the pages with the key dates on and around the times of the killings. The crew picked up a leather jacket and red scarf from his closet, among other effects. The fibers from the scarf matched those found on Hammerer's body. A pile of gas and restaurant receipts reaffirmed that Jack had been in the vicinity of several of the murders. The noose of guilt had tightened.

At Jack's request, Bianca wired her mother for money. Mrs. Mrak knew her daughter was in trouble. She advised the Austrian authorities that her Bianca was in Miami.

In a sting operation, *Success Magazine* offered Jack $10,000 for an on-the-run article. The editor agreed to send a check in advance of the interview as a sign of good faith.

Like a stag pushing the doe across the road ahead of him to protect himself, Jack ordered Bianca to pick up the envelope. She entered the USA Money Exchange Office on Eleventh Street in South Beach on February 27, 1992. As she left the building, U.S. Marshal Shawn Conboy and his team of deputies arrested her.

Unterweger watched from across the street as the authorities took his fiancée into custody. He bolted through a restaurant and into a parking lot in an effort to escape. The deputies quickly apprehended and handcuffed the fleeing Austrian. When he asked why he had been stopped, the agents explained that the arrest had come about due to his illegal entry into the states. Thinking he avoided more serious charges, he joked that the deputies might appear in his next book. When he discovered they also took him as a suspect for murder, he broke down and cried.

In fear for her freedom, Bianca cooperated with the United States lawmen. She took them to the apartment she and Jack shared after they had checked out of their fleabag hotel room. When the authorities searched it, they confiscated Unterweger's journal, which contained evidence that he had considered killing Bianca.

Forensic testing of Unterweger's bodily fluids tied him to one of the Los Angeles murders. Detective Fred Miller flew to Miami to question the prisoner. Unterweger exuded confidence. He admitted staying at the Cecil and having sex with one white and two Latina prostitutes but feigned ignorance about the three murders. Although Jack's DNA matched that taken from one Los Angeles victim, her body contained traces of semen from other customers.

The LAPD employed the assistance of FBI profiler Jim McMurray, who examined twelve boxes of evidence. McMurray added his input, employing the Violent Criminal Apprehension Computer Analysis (VICA) from ten thousand cases and fifteen criteria to connect Unterweger to the Los Angeles murders.

Still lacking conclusive evidence to guarantee a conviction, the United States legal team allowed Unterweger's May 28, 1992 deportation into the Austrian criminal system. The choice pleased Jack, since Austria eschewed the death penalty. When he landed under guard in Vienna, Unterweger faced the media at the airport with bravado, asserting his innocence.

The Austrian judicial process differs vastly from that of the United States. A three-judge panel, a jury of eight, rather than twelve, the prosecutor, the defense team and even the defendant maintained the right to pose questions. The jury's verdict required a majority rather than a unanimous vote. Since Austria had eliminated the death penalty, life in prison represented the maximum possible sentence for murder.

The trial for eleven murders opened in Graz on April 20, 1994, coincidentally, the date of Adolf Hitler's birthday. Psychiatrist Dr. Reinhard Haller presented his diagnosis to the jury; he said Unterweger was a man suffering from advanced narcissistic personality disorder. The prosecution brought forth forensic scientists and FBI experts to prove their case. The similarities in the technique of the murders, the defendant's proximity to the crime scenes and a raft of strong circumstantial evidence, including DNA and threads from Jack's clothing found on victims, attested to Unterweger's involvement. Although the state provided no direct proof or witnesses, few doubted the certainty of Unterweger's guilt.

Like the splendid actor he was, Jack played to the gallery in a final plea, employing his boyish charm and manipulative skills. He arose and orated:

> *I was a rat, a primitive criminal who grunted rather than talked, an inveterate liar. The prosecution is right. I consumed women rather than loved them....I am counting on your acquittal, because I am not the culprit. Your decision will not only affect me, but the real killer, who is laughing up his sleeve.*[36]

While the jury deliberated Jack's innocence or guilt, a bomb exploded outside the courthouse. Nonetheless, debate continued, uninterrupted. After a trial of more than two months, the jury voted six to two to convict Unterweger on nine counts of murder. Due to the severe decomposition camouflaging the cause of death for two of the bodies, the jury refused to present a ruling on the deaths of Regina Prem and Elfriede Schrempf.

The Tuesday, June 29, 1995 guilty verdict arrived with a clap of thunder and a burst of lightning as a storm raked the exterior of the courtroom. Even nature applauded the trial's outcome: a sentence of life in prison without the possibility of parole. At last, the murders would end—or that is what the prosecution assumed.

That evening, Jack Unterweger entered his Graz-Karau prison cell and wept. Guards checked on him at 3:00 a.m. He lay on his cot, asleep. When they checked an hour later, they discovered him hanging from a curtain rod. He had improvised the signature ligature he used to kill prostitutes in his own suicide. A noose constructed from a cord on his trousers did the trick. One of those who knew him considered Unterweger's final murder, his own, as his best killing of all.

Unterweger's poetry foretold his own epitaph:

> *You still seem strange and distant and lively, Death,*
> *But one day you will be close and full of flames.*
> *Come, lover, I am yours.*[37]

Like with his Hotel Cecil predecessor Richard Ramirez, the Night Stalker, a cult followed this international serial killer. In 2008, actor John Malkovich portrayed Unterweger's life in a performance play, *Seduction and Despair*, which premiered at Barnum Hall in Santa Monica. He presented a fully staged version in Vienna in 2009, titled *The Infernal Comedy*.

In 2015, Elisabeth Scharang directed the Austrian film *Jack*, starring Johannes Krishna. Broad Green Pictures announced the preproduction of a film based on John Leake's book *Entering Hades* with actor Michael Fassbender. Season 2, episode 14 of *The FBI Files* related the story of Unterweger's capture, and *Biography* described his atrocities in "Poet of Death." Discovery Channel's true crime series *Horror at the Cecil Hotel*, aired on October 16, 2017, presented the Unterweger story. In January 2021, the Discovery Plus Channel premiered a show about the Cecil Hotel, with paranormalists sensing the evil vibes that emanated from Unterweger's former room.

In any case, the myth of death and horror surrounding the Cecil exploded with the fact that not one but two serial killers used the hotel as their base of operations. In the years ahead, another strange event would secure the Cecil's position as the city's and perhaps the world's eeriest hotel.

THE MYSTERIOUS DEATH
OF ELISA LAM

Perhaps the Cecil's greatest enigma involved the death and disappearance of twenty-one-year-old Asian American Elisa Lam (Lam Ho Yi in Cantonese). She was born in Vancouver, Canada, on April 30, 1991, to immigrants from Hong Hong who ran a Chinese restaurant named Paul's.

In school, she performed well academically, taking senior classes while still in the eighth grade. She liked to read, lapping up all the age-appropriate literature she could: *Catcher in the Rye*, *The Outsiders* and, her favorite, *The Great Gatsby*. Although she was only a mediocre athlete at best, she participated in cross-country. Her classmates considered her a loner, but she took part in student council and appeared to be well liked.

Outwardly, Elisa appeared much like every other typical teenage girl. Inside, depression attacked her. Dark moods often clouded her mind. Some mornings, a heaviness in her heart made it difficult for Elisa to get out of bed and start the day. This horrible burden crippled her ability to enjoy a normal life.

In the twelfth grade, she dropped cross-country for volleyball, a team sport. She received little game time, and the coach told her at the end of the season that he felt sorry she played so little. She left the gym in tears, knowing that dropping track had been another wrong choice in a life filled with bad decisions.

By the end of her twelfth-grade year, Elisa believed her friends had betrayed her. Her illness isolated her from her classmates. She complained online about her own behavior: "I have no filter. My mouth is my downfall."

As Elisa's despair intensified, she wrote two quotes, summing up her inner sadness:

"There is no physical manifestation of my 'illness.' Would I become psychotic and want to off myself? I'm too much of a coward. Instead, I'll just lie in my bed and let the days pass by."

Depression is "the most debilitating, humiliating disease I have ever been subjected to. It makes a fool of you. It sucks out every shard of hope or motivation that you ever had in your body, and it makes you want to destroy yourself."[38]

Elisa substituted social networking for human interaction. Blogspot hosted her site, *Ether Fields*, where she asked, "Why don't I simply do the things that I know will make me better?"[39]

The internet served as Elisa's confidant, her diary, her best friend and her spiritual backbone. She poured out her heart online and found solace. Although she had used Facebook, toyed with Pinterest for fashion designs, tried YouTube and tested Instagram and Twitter, Tumblr served as her social media favorite. The internet also presented her with the vehicle to research new clothing styles, a pet pursuit that she blogged about on her Tumblr site *Nouvelle-Nouveau*.

Death imprinted a lasting tattoo on Elisa. The loss of her puppy to a speeding car sunk her into melancholy. When her grandfather died from failing kidneys shortly thereafter, her depression grew intolerable. Bipolar sufferers sometimes think about suicide, but Elisa expressed no interest in harming herself. She just experienced continual gloom. Like Joe Btfsplk, the sad sack, Al Capp *Li'l Abner* cartoon character, a gray cloud always hung over her head.

On September 12, 2012, she posted: "I want to kill myself....I see no purpose in living anymore. I'm waiting for this to pass, and tomorrow it will hopefully be gone."[40]

Doctors prescribed Venlafaxine, a selective serotonin-norepinephrine-reuptake inhibitor (SSNRI), to smooth out her bipolar moods and control depression. Sometimes it helped. Doctors later added Wellbutrin, Lamictal, Seroquel and Effexor.

Elisa entered the University of British Columbia following her graduation from high school, but her mental health handicapped her ability to keep up with the required schoolwork. In December 2011, she dropped two classes. She overslept one day, missing a big test that counted for 10 percent of her year's grade. She stayed up most of the night, baring her soul on Tumblr, rather than studying and sleeping.

Elisa's self-control needed a boost. Her personal prescription involved a break from school and Vancouver to revive her sanity. A healthy dose of adventure might generate the ideal change of pace to jar her from her lethargy—but only if her parents allowed. She promised her mom to check in every night and to be careful if her dad fronted the funds to visit California. She beamed with anticipation when she received parental permission.

Elisa took off in late January 2013 via Amtrak for San Diego to drink in Southern California's culture. She spent a day at the city's world-famous zoo and toured the sights: Balboa Park, the art museum and old town. She posted pictures of her escapades on social media. As promised, she faithfully called her parents every evening to provide a review of the day's highlights.

On Saturday, January 26, Elisa attended a midnight speakeasy show. When she returned to her hotel, she discovered the loss of her Blackberry phone. Luckily, she still had her laptop. On Monday, January 28, she boarded the Amtrak train north to Los Angeles, where she registered at the Cecil Hotel for a shared dormitory-style room with two other single women. She took a day trip of the city on January 29 and attended a taping of the *Conan O'Brien* television show on January 30. The medical expert Dr. Sanjay Gupta, a personal favorite of Elisa's, appeared as Conan's guest celebrity. The television show *The Vanishing* reported that Elisa's strange behavior forced ushers to escort her out of the taping.

After two nights at the Cecil, Elisa's roommates on the community bunk floor complained about her weird ways. They discovered notes on their pillows reading, "Stay away," which frightened them. Management transferred Elisa to room 412, a single, on January 31. Her scheduled itinerary involved a departure to Santa Cruz the following day, Friday, February 1.

Late in the day, Elisa shopped for gifts for her sister and parents at the Last Bookstore, the onetime home of Crocker Bank. Manager Katie Orphan waited on her and thought she seemed upbeat and pleasant. Another customer, Tosh Berman, who was shopping for records, spoke with her as well. His opinion differed. She appeared overly trusting, more so than a young single woman should be in a transitional neighborhood. Her demeanor made him uncomfortable: "I was worried because she seemed mentally unwell."[41] Berman, a TamTam books publisher, referred to Skid Row as the "Gates of Hell." He recognized its potential dangers and feared for Elisa's safety. Girls like her could be susceptible to predators. These two witnesses with different viewpoints appeared to be the last people to speak with her.

The Last Bookstore, Los Angeles. *Image from Wikimedia Commons.*

Elisa failed to call home on January 31 as she had done every other evening. Her family asked the hotel to check her room. Her ID card, purse and clothing appeared intact, but Elisa had disappeared. Within a day, authorities initiated a hunt.

However, other legal concerns slowed the intensity of the quest. The Elisa Lam search took a distant second to tracking down cop-killer, former naval officer and ex-policeman Christopher Dorner. After being terminated for filing an excessive force charge against his training officer, Dorner, a Black man, appealed the ruling, citing racism. He lost. Totally unhinged, he issued a manifesto against the LAPD.

On February 3, Dorner murdered Monica Quan, the daughter of a police captain, along with her fiancé, Keith Lawrence. Two other law enforcement murders followed. With an all-hands-on-deck mentality, the police pursued Dorner until they boxed him inside a cabin near the resort area of Big Bear. After he refused the call to surrender, the police shot pyrotechnic tear gas canisters into his hiding place. When the building roared with fire, Dorner killed himself with a single bullet to the head on February 12. With that case ended, police concentrated all their investigative efforts on the hunt for Elisa.

Teams had already scoured the hotel for the missing girl. Tracking dogs inspected the hallways of every floor and the roof, seeking her scent, but without luck. Elisa Lam had disappeared.

Left: Christopher Dorner. *Image from an LAPD handout.*

Middle: Elisa Lam. *Image from an LAPD missing person notice.*

Right: Elisa Lam in the elevator. *Image from Wikimedia Commons.*

Elisa's sister and parents arrived in Los Angeles to assist. After several days, the police and the family held a formal press conference, requesting public assistance. Detectives released a video of Elisa from the Cecil's fourteenth-floor elevator camera. Newsman Dennis Romero posted it on YouTube, where it received millions of views.

The hazy, closed-caption, four-minute elevator surveillance video showed Elisa engaged in some crazy trauma. Her staggered steps and stares signaled a preternatural fear as if some demon had possessed her. She randomly punched floor buttons and lurched in and out of the elevator, apparently on one of the residential floors rather than the lobby. Some wondered if she had been playing the "Elevator Game," a ritual where a person entered a number of floors in an attempt to enter another dimension.

Elisa peeked around the corner as if someone had been following her and gesticulated with her hands and arms like a symphony conductor raising the orchestra's tempo to a crescendo. At times, the camera showed her playing hide and go seek. Had depression, fear, a supernatural force or a combination of the three overtaken her?

Web sleuths questioned if more videos might be available. Detective Wallace Tennelle corroborated that additional footage existed. Supposedly, one showed Elisa at the elevator with two men, who handed her a box, but nothing about it had been released to the public. The television show *The Vanishing* indicated that the men had actually worked at the Last Bookstore and delivered the gifts Elisa had purchased.

While the hunt for Elisa intensified, Cecil manager Amy Price received numerous gripes concerning the hotel's water quality and pressure. That very day, two more residents called. When occupant Steven Cott marched to the front desk to lodge a formal complaint, Price recognized a serious problem might indeed exist. Cecil lodgers accepted a lower quality of service and cleanliness than that provided by the upscale Biltmore or the swanky Ritz Carlton. They willingly exchanged amenities and an iffy area for reasonable rates, but they expected safe and clean water.

Mr. Cott said his tap water oozed from the faucets with a sickly-sweet odor. The sludge made a warm shower impossible, and he had no interest in brushing his teeth in so foul a liquid. Price recognized that water pollution might create serious, even lethal, consequences. The problem demanded immediate attention.

Amy dispatched maintenance worker Santiago Lopez, a three-year Cecil veteran, to check out the problem right away. He had plenty to do that Tuesday, February 19, but his boss had declared this water situation a priority. He intended to investigate the complaints room by room. The resident in 320 claimed the low water pressure made it impossible to rinse the shampoo from his hair. With Lopez unable to speed the flow, the tenant scowled, but Santiago promised in broken English to come up with a solution. Room 720 presented a similar issue.

Lopez knocked on room 451. He held a superstitious streak. His coworkers told him a suicide had occurred in this very room. Several years ago, a room 451 resident awoke in the middle of the night with the sensation that some invisible force had choked him. He ran to the front desk in a cold sweat, demanding another room. When he was told none was available, he checked out of the hotel in a huff. Lopez discovered no strangler, just low water pressure.

A woman in 943 named Natalie asked him to run the tub. Although the water ran clearly, the tub's red stains confirmed her story. Out of the blue, the woman asked if anyone had died in the room. Lopez blithely remarked that someone had probably died in every room.

Santiago took the elevator to the top floor to check out the water supply. Using his key, he bypassed the alarm system and ambled onto the roof to check the cisterns. If anyone had attempted to go on to the roof without proper permission, a noisy alarm at the front desk and on the two top floors would signal the entry. Santiago later testified under oath that the alarm operated perfectly that day.

The roof contained four one-thousand-gallon cylindrical containers supplying water to the residents through a gravity-based system. Each tower stood ten feet tall and six feet in diameter on top of a platform raised four feet above ground level.

Santiago climbed the steps to the platform and scaled a second ladder attached to one of the tanks. As he reached the top, he noticed that one of the heavy eighteen-inch-square lids stood open. He wondered if the police had left it that way when they searched for the missing girl. Dusting off his pants and stabilizing his balance, the maintenance worker peered inside the tank. What he saw terrified him. "*Dios mio!*" he exclaimed in Spanish. Something red in the vat grabbed his attention. The body of a dead woman with a swollen and protruding eye stared up at him from beneath the water.

Santiago inhaled and crossed himself. He immediately contacted his supervisor and the front desk. Around ten in the morning, the police received a call from management and dispatched officers to investigate. Elisa's clothes floated throughout the tank: a pair of black shorts, a size large green shirt with an Alexander Keith India Pale Ale logo, a shirt with a deer logo, sandals, black-trimmed underwear and an extra-small red hoodie.

In the early afternoon, the fire department arrived and sliced open the tank with lasers to spill out the liquid and remove the naked body from its watery grave. The authorities took the body of the deceased to the Forensic Science Center for an autopsy. Later that day, Elisa's family identified her.

As five-foot-four-inch-tall, 115-pound Elisa lay on the table for examining, she appeared bloated and waxen. The forensic team noted a one-inch scar on her right knee and a quarter-inch abrasion on her left knee. They found no visible sign of trauma. Her waterlogged hands and feet appeared wrinkled and misshapen due to spending more than two weeks in the tank. A wrist watch and hotel key card lay next to her.

Preliminary results of the autopsy appeared on February 27. The examiners initially listed "accident" as the cause of death. The coroner's office refused to release a full toxicology report until June 19, nearly four months later, an inordinately long delay. Lam's body contained no illicit drugs, only small amounts of the expected antidepressant and antipsychotic inhibitors a doctor would prescribe for bipolar disorder.

The autopsy showed a pooling of blood in the victim's anal area. This might indicate sexual abuse or may merely be the result of the body's decomposition.

Someone in the office crossed out the preliminary finding of "accident" on the autopsy report as the cause of death and replaced it with "could not be determined." On June 21, pathologist Yulai Wang scratched out "could not be determined" and replaced it again with a box marked "accident."

Although Dr. Wang's autopsy result ended the official inquest, web sleuths and conspiracy theorists instituted their own investigations. Many unanswered questions still remained.

Cecil residents had raged about the vile-tasting and dangerous tap water for more than two weeks. Eighty-nine-year-old long-term guest Bernard Calvin

Diaz only learned of the problem while listening to the news on television. He told a reporter: "So many things have happened in this place that nothing surprises me."[42] Diaz had lived at the Cecil since February 1, 1993.

Mike and Sabina Baugh, tourists from Plymouth, England, came to the Cecil for their first vacation in the United States. A budget provider had put their trip together. Even though their expectations had been modest, the room's tattered and dusty appearance disappointed them. They had brushed their teeth and swigged the foul water from the spigot. The brown sludge shocked and disgusted them, especially after they learned its source.

The Los Angeles director of public health stated the chlorine in the water probably reduced the potential for disease. Cecil's management provided bottled water and ordered everyone to avoid drinking or showering until they could give the all-clear. The Cecil took the cistern offline for repair and decontamination. During the next few days, fifty-five booked guests marched out of the Cecil's doors to seek housing elsewhere.

Steven and Gloria Cott filed a class action suit for the return of $150 for a two-night stay, $100 for medical costs and attorney's fees. The courts denied their claim and refused to find fault with the hotel.

Multiple explanations surrounded and compounded the questions regarding Elisa Lam's death, some far more plausible than others. Was her demise an accident, murder, suicide, a product of mental illness, the result of paranormal activity or some combination? Each theory maintained its own adherents. To paraphrase Winston Churchill's description of Russia, Lam's death was "a riddle wrapped in a mystery inside an enigma." A newscaster stated that the public knew the where, what and when, but the how and why required answers.

The cistern lid proved especially confusing. If it had been open, as Santiago claimed, why would the police have failed to check the cistern when they searched the roof? If the lid had been closed, this would indicate foul play. Officer Andrew Smith, one of the first LAPD officers to appear on the scene, thought the tank lid had been closed when he arrived. If Smith's recollection proved correct, why would Santiago or anyone else alter a potential crime scene?

Could there have been a coverup? Author Jake Anderson discussed an odd issue with the timing of the elevator video. "At approximately 2:42, the minute hand of the time code changed. Seven seconds elapse and then, at 2:49, the minute hand changed again. The minute hand changes twice in seven seconds."[43] Had someone doctored the tape?

Other issues led to debate. Why had the autopsy taken so long? What changed the cause of death from accident to undetermined and back to accident again? Although the autopsy team had gathered rape kit evidence, Deputy Coroner Fred Corral stated that processing had never been completed due to cost considerations.

What would make a single woman wander around the hotel? Why would she go to the fourteenth floor when her room was on the fourth? Long-term guests, rather than transients, generally lived on the upper floors.

Residents did not trust the security staff, which had a bad reputation. One older guest named Sally locked her door every night and blocked it with her flipped-over wheelchair to provide added protection. When Sally heard about Elisa's death, she assumed the girl had been murdered. Could a hotel security worker with a passkey have accompanied her to the roof and forced himself on her?

Dr. John Hiserodt of Path Lab Services, a processor of medical tests and an experienced autopsy expert, questioned the cause of death. "In a drowning case, most victims have voluminous fluid in their lungs….They breathe the water, and that's how you die; the lungs are heavy…and full of water. In the Elisa Lam case, there was no water in the lungs."[44]

Dr. Hiserodt provided a possible explanation. In a small number of cases, about 15 percent, dry drownings occur. The larynx locks, and the victim cannot inhale water or breathe. Drowning deaths, either wet or dry, usually lead to water in the intricate cavities behind the nose. Apparently, the examiner failed to check this.

There seemed to have been little evidence that the police questioned Elisa's two former Cecil roommates from room 506. They surely could have provided valuable information on her state of mind.

Elisa's high school classmate Alex Ristea considered her to be one of the nicest and friendliest people he knew. He could not imagine she died by suicide. University of British Columbia confirmed that Elisa had attended summer school, but at that time, she had not registered in any classes.

Paranormalists pointed to the supernatural playing a role in Elisa Lam's death. In Jake Anderson's book *Gone at Midnight*, the author cited guest Natalie Davis, a psychic medium who stayed on the same floor as the 1962 suicide victim Pauline Otton: "I had a very uneasy feeling. I walked over to the window, and the first thought that came to my mind was, 'Wow, if I wanted to kill myself, I could just open this window and jump.' At this point, I'm convinced that that thought was sort of 'inserted' into my head."[45] Could spirits, some dark presence or a force of evil have compelled Elisa to jump into the tank?

In the show *Lam to the Slaughter: Dark History, Dark Water*, radio host Clyde Lewis discussed the "synchronicity of evil," the conglomeration of strange deaths and unexplained events that occurred at the Cecil over the decades.

Elisa's Tumblr account posted a quote from author Virginia Wolfe months after her death. Over the next year, other random images and messages appeared out of the blue on her site. Web sleuths questioned how this happened.

Jake Anderson provided a host of conspiracy theories without endorsing any. He mentioned that witchcraft celebrates the holy day of Imbolc on February 1. Had Elisa Lam served as a Satanic sacrifice?

Strangely, the Last Bookstore's website registrar address, V5G4S2, translated on Google maps to Elisa's hometown of Burnaby, British Columbia. The city's center point landed squarely at the cemetery where Elisa had been buried. This may be a coincidence, but many sleuths refuse to ignore the so-called synchronicity surrounding Elisa Lam's death.

Of course, logic tells us other far more realist explanations abound. A manic episode may very well have impelled Elisa to carry out suicide, possibly brought on by her solitude in a strange hotel.

Other theories pointed to murder. Four former sex offenders resided in the Cecil Hotel, and another half dozen lived within a few blocks. Elisa's friend Joe Elwell, who worked summers with her at the Pacific National Exhibition, provided his opinion. "There's no way in hell her death was an accident."[46] Joe described Elisa as a girl with a smile that could light up a room. However, Joe knew nothing about her struggles with depression.

Ama McDonald, a University of New Brunswick graduate with a number of filmmaking credits, remained in postproduction of a documentary on the Cecil. After interviewing several residents, he leaned toward murder as the cause of Elisa Lam's death.

A former resident called Dred, mentioned by Jake Anderson, accused security of involvement in the killing. Could she have been dead already and dropped into the tank by her killer or killers? Elisa's death left dozens of questions but no firm answers.

However, like Occam's Razor, the law of parsimony, the simplest explanation generally remains the right one. That would lead us to believe that Elisa Lam killed herself during a manic episode. Apparently, she had slowed down her intake of her meds, which could have led to disastrous results.

The 2002 Japanese movie *Dark Waters* and its 2005 American remake provide a premonition of Elisa Lam's death. The films feature a young girl,

Ceci (an allusion to the Cecil), dressed in a red coat (reminiscent of Elisa's red hoodie), falling into a water tank and drowning. The contaminated water flows into the bathrooms of the building, just as it had at the Cecil. Both films feature elevator scenes and erratic behavior. The American version even has a character named Dahlia, a reminder of Elizabeth Short, the Black Dahlia.

In 2013, Skid Row experienced a serious outbreak of tuberculosis, especially virulent among the homeless. The Center for Disease Control (CDC) estimated the disease might have affected as many as 4,500 locals. The medical teams employed a diagnostic test called "Lam-Elisa," another strange coincidence.

In 2014, Sony announced the preproduction of a movie titled *The Bringing*, based on Brandon and Phillip Murray's script about Elisa Lam's death, which occurred a few days before World Bipolar Awareness Day. The producers lined up Jeremy Lovering as the director and Michael Peña as a lead. Two years later, Sony dropped the project, which now remains in the development stage.

On November 3, 2015, Elisa's parents, David and Yinna Lam, filed a motion against the Cecil for wrongful negligence, alleging "hotel operators had an obligation to inspect and seek out hazards that presented an unreasonable risk of danger to their daughter and other hotel guests."[47] The plaintiffs' attorneys, Thomas Johnston and Brian Needelman, represented the family at the downtown Stanley Mosk Courthouse for case number BC521927, *Lam vs. the Cecil*.

Maintenance man Santiago Lopez testified at a preliminary deposition that the cistern door had been open when he investigated. Following the trial, Lopez quit his job and disappeared to parts unknown in Mexico. Those who were seeking further information on the case failed to locate him.

Lopez's boss, chief engineer Pedro Tovar, testified that the alarm system to the roof had been in good working condition and, to the best of his knowledge, had not been breached. Interestingly, management elevated Tovar to the hotel board of directors shortly thereafter. He explained that Elisa could only have reached the roof by climbing one of the three exterior fire escapes. Company policy forbade guests from accessing the roof. After reviewing the facts, Judge Howard Halm dismissed the Lams' case.

Like almost everyone else connected to the case, Jake Anderson, the author of *Gone at Midnight*, discussed a slew of theories but lacked concrete answers. However, he wrote: "When I first started writing this book, I deferred more

The Cecil Hotel, 2005. *Courtesy of Jim Winstead, Creative Commons.*

to the reality of mental illness and believed that to be the more likely cause for her being discovered in the water tank. However, based on the evidence I've uncovered, I now believe it is more likely that Elisa was not alone on the roof and that something unexpected happened involving other people; furthermore, it's more likely Elisa was not alive when she entered the water tank….Based on the evidence, I am convinced that something criminal was and is being covered up….So then, what the hell happened? Much to my dismay, I don't know."[48] Without a doubt, the Elisa Lam case lacked a degree of transparency and deserved more investigation. However, I lean toward an accidental death during a psychotic episode.

The mystery has continued to tantalize the public. The season-three episode of the *NoSleep Podcast*, titled "The Cecil Hotel," adapted a fictional horror tale based loosely on the Elisa Lam case. The gaming studio Acck released *YIIK*, a postmodern role-playing game (RPG), with noted similarities to the Lam case. One scene takes place in an elevator, revealing an alternate dimension.

ABC's *How to Get Away with Murder* portrays the death of a sorority girl whose body ends up in a cistern. In the show, a maintenance worker discovers the deceased due to a drop in water pressure. *Hungry Ghost Ritual*, a thriller, mimicks the Lam elevator scene.

In January 2021, a Discovery Plus *Ghost Adventures* television show on the Cecil emphasized the psychic energy generated by the mysterious girl in the cistern case. As late as February 10, 2021, a Netflix program titled *Crime Scene: The Vanishing at the Cecil Hotel* took another shot at the Elisa Lam mystery.

Elisa Lam also impacted the music videos of Pablo Vergara (better known as Morbid), the Zolas, Hail the Sun and Sun Kil Moon. The haunting lyrics of Hail the Sun's "Disappearing Syndrome" reinforce the psychic import of the Cecil:

> *Nightmares! Some come true.*
> *Never let your guard down.*
> *No one is immune.*
> *Anything that can will happen.*
> *Such is the story lived through Elisa,*
> *Stuck in time.*
>
> *Checking into the hotel taunted by the building itself*
> *And I wonder if the walls spoke,*
> *Would they share the cruelest dreams?*
> *Would they tell about the murders in the bedrooms?*
> *Or of suicide by jumping out of their rooms?*
> *Or the stalker on the top floor?*
> *Don't go looking, don't go looking!*

The obsession surrounding Elisa Lam's questionable death continues to this day and has provided yet another piece of validation for the armies of paranormalists and conspiracy theorists who cite the Cecil as America's most terrifying hotel.

8

HOTEL SUICIDE

Throughout the years—both before and after the times of Richard Ramirez, Jack Unterweger and Elisa Lam—suicides, robberies and strange happenings occurred with frequency at the Cecil. In November 1947, thirty-five-year-old Robert Smith of 1144 Gladys Street in Long Beach jumped or fell from a window on the seventh floor to his death. Little else is known concerning the suicide. Apparently, the spirit of the Cecil had cast its shadow across another victim.

A befuddled fifty-year-old Alexander M. Galbraith telephoned a friend back east to complain of being stranded at the Cecil Hotel in Los Angeles. He had no idea how he got there or why. Galbraith had worked the last four years of his life as the honorary British consul in Pittsburgh, Pennsylvania. Although his job primarily involved routine issues, such as lost or stolen passports, form renewals, visa applications and changes in status due to birth, marriage or death, he relished the job.

Suddenly and inexplicably, on Saturday, January 3, 1948, Galbraith's superiors terminated him from his "temporary" status as a consul, a position he had intended to continue. Shocked by his unexpected ouster, he left his office in a fog, a victim of amnesia.

Galbraith failed to remember how he left Pittsburgh. He recalled stopping in Canton, Ohio, and Chicago, but how he arrived at the Cecil Hotel or even Los Angeles remained a mystery. Nearly a month of his life disappeared from his consciousness. He had no idea where it went—another puzzle tucked into the Cecil Hotel's files of the inexplicable.

On December 14, 1949, twenty-four-year-old Wake Forrest College predental student Raymond D. Hair lost $400 in a card game. He wrote out a check to the biggest winner, Watson Coble, in a play for time. When the check bounced, Coble demanded his money. The two drove in a car and argued when a gun appeared; the twenty-year-old Coble died from a bullet wound to the head.

Hair raced home, snatched $325 from his family's basement and fled from North Carolina, through Washington, D.C., to Las Vegas and on to Los Angeles, where he registered at the Cecil Hotel as J.S. Roster. Based on a tip, the police burst into his room on January 12 and arrested the sleeping Hair. The perpetrator offered no resistance and admitted he was trying to work up the courage to go home and "face the music." He owned a single suit, an extra shirt and $165 in cash when he was taken to the station. The authorities extradited him to Raleigh. Three months later, a judge sentenced him to twenty-five years in prison for second-degree murder. In 1955, Hair received parole for exemplary behavior.

In February 1950, Ed Baughman of Monrovia lost an arm at the Cecil in a horrific elevator accident. The injured victim sued. Superior court judge Caryl Sheldon issued a verdict of $31,042 in favor of the plaintiff as restitution. The defendants in the case included the Cecil Hotel; the hotel's new management company, Junior Realty; and its chief executive officer Ben Weingart.

Junior Realty provided the bank holding the Cecil's shaky loans with an opportunity to cut its ties and stem the flow of red ink. Weingart's company oversaw the day-to-day operations for a percentage of the rents and some form of ownership, just as it had done for a number of other distressed properties. Mr. Weingart recognized that even in the worst of times, people sought clean, cheap shelter, and his company possessed the necessary know-how to operate a hotel professionally and economically. With limited alternatives, the banks accepted multimillionaire Weingart's package to avoid full receivership.

Having earned a fortune in downtown hotels like the Cecil, Ben Weingart through his Weingart Foundation donated $125,000 in 1979 to the Volunteers of America (VOA) in support of the Skid Row Detoxification and Rehabilitation Center. In 1980, Junior Realty and its failing, ninety-two-year-old founder deeded the 621-room El Rey Hotel on San Pedro and Sixth Streets to the VOA for use as an indigent alcoholic rehab retreat called the Weingart Center. In addition, the foundation donated $1 million to upgrade the elevators and building structure. Another $100,000 grant from the

Weingart Foundation a few years later, following its founder's passing, helped provide childcare facilities for the poor. Indirectly, the Cecil's philanthropic owner had returned much of his earnings to downtown's neediest.

A cast of do-gooders like Weingart failed to halt the deterioration surrounding Skid Row. As the area worsened, bad things continued to happen at the Cecil. A woman quietly registered for room 704 at the Cecil as Margaret Brown of Denver. One week later, on October 22, 1954, she jumped from her seventh-floor window to her death, crashing atop the marquee. Police, firemen and an ambulance sped to the scene, sirens blaring.

Firemen raised a ladder, climbed to the top of the entryway and lowered the bloody and broken form to the ground. The gruesome thump of the body slamming into the building and the removal of the deceased unnerved a bystander, twenty-eight-year-old Melvin Hankley of 227 Olive Street, who ran screaming into the auditorium of a nearby public building. The police calmed his histrionics, fearful that he might harm himself or others, taking him to General Hospital for observation.

When detectives went through the deceased's purse, identification cards yielded her true name, Helen C. Gurnee, a fifty-five-year-old stationery clerk from San Francisco. Few other details have surfaced.

With the Cecil's scandals brought to light through the media's reporting of arrests and deaths, the hotel's occupancy rates nosedived. The Cecil twisted and turned in a swirl of debt, one rogue wave away from utter financial ruin. A September 3, 1961 newspaper advertisement sought potential guests by offering a desperation rate of only $10.50 per week.

Julia Frances Moore, age fifty, jumped from her eighth-floor window, landing on the second-floor interior light well on February 11, 1962, another in the hotel's long list of suicides. A check of Julia Moore's purse produced just $0.59 in change, a used bus ticket from St. Louis to Los Angeles and a Springfield, Illinois bank book containing a balance of $1,800.00, worth nearly $16,000.00 today. Her room contained a small overnight bag. Detective Sergeant Paul LePage found no sign of foul play and intended to check the two St. Louis addresses he discovered among her effects for additional information.

On October 12, 1962, twenty-seven-year-old Pauline Otton of 504 West Forty-First Drive argued violently with her estranged husband, Dewey, a sheet metal worker. In a huff, Mr. Otton informed his wife that he planned to leave her for good. He barged out of the door and slammed it in his wife's face. Tears poured down Pauline's face. With little left to keep her alive, she penned a hasty suicide note and laid it on the nightstand. Pauline slid open the window of her ninth-floor room and leaped to her death, but the death took a strange twist.

Pauline Otton landed on sixty-five-year-old pedestrian George Gianinni, formerly of 440 West Third Street, who happened to be in the wrong place at the wrong time; they were both killed instantly. Since the police found no witnesses, they initially assumed the pair had jumped out the window together in a suicide pact. However, an inspection of Gianinni's corpse demonstrated that his hands remained inside his pockets and his shoes on his feet, proof he could not have jumped. Otherwise, his shoes would have flown off, and his hands would have been outstretched from the force of the fall.

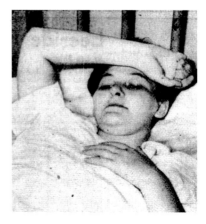

Dorothy Jean Purcell threw her baby boy down twelve stories to his death. *Image from the* LA Times, *1944.*

The April 12, 1963 *Californian* reported the death of sixty-five-year-old Delbert Lawrence, who jumped from the fourteenth floor into the parking lot behind the Cecil Hotel. No other information appeared.

On the afternoon of June 4, 1964, a hotel employee who was delivering phone books rapped on the door of room 1016. When the occupant failed to answer the knock, she inserted her passkey and entered. As she dropped the book on the floor, she gasped. Her eyes latched onto the bloody and battered body of a popular six-year-resident, seventy-nine-year-old "Pigeon Goldie" Osgood, a retired telephone operator.[49] In a matter of minutes, the police received a frantic call for help.

An investigator determined the killer had stuffed a rag in the victim's mouth before beating, raping and stabbing her to death. The room had been ransacked. A paper bag filled with birdseed and the blue Dodgers baseball cap Goldie habitually wore lay beside her body.

A few hours after the murder, the authorities nabbed twenty-nine-year-old Jacques Ehlinger in Pershing Park, near Goldie's favorite bench where she fed her birds. Although Ehlinger admitted he knew the deceased, had bloodstains on his clothing and left fingerprints on the park bench, an alibi eliminated him as a suspect.

Friends of Goldie, headed up by retired nurse Jean Rosenstein, collected money for a floral memorial. Most tenants lacked spare cash, but everyone

Goldie Osgood. *Image from the* LA Times, *1964*.

shared what little they had. Goldie's neighbors wanted to be sure she would be remembered.

The police connected the Osgood murder to that of fifty-year-old victim Viva Brown, who died in a nearby hotel the previous May. Both crimes remain unsolved.

On February 10, 1971, the Cecil reappeared in the news when an earthquake shattered its windows on the seventh floor. Guest Gerrit Arens advised a *Los Angeles Times* reporter that he feared for his life when the tremor intensified. Although the shaking rattled his nerves, the hotel suffered minimal damage, and Arens had no injuries.

On December 20, 1975, an unidentified woman, approximately twenty-three years of age, jumped from a twelfth-floor window onto the Cecil's second-floor roof. The victim had registered into room 327 under the alias

"Allison Lowell." She stood five feet, four inches tall and weighed about 118 pounds. She had brown hair and hazel eyes with notable scars on her wrists, a possible indication of a previous suicide attempt. She wore a blue sweater and navy slacks. Her dresser drawer held a used December 15 Greyhound bus ticket to Los Angeles from Bakersfield. The jumper's purse contained a gold key but no identification. Her real name remains unknown. Hotel Suicide had struck again.

On December 2, 1976, police arrested twenty-six-year-old Jeffrey Thomas Paley at the Cecil after he fired more than a dozen shots from a .22 rifle into a bank building from the roof of the hotel. Paley had just purchased the rifle without undergoing a background check or answering any questions. He explained that he wanted to demonstrate the ease by which a former mental patient could obtain a lethal weapon. Since the shooting occurred late at night, Paley assumed the bank would be empty. Actually, an employee remained on duty at the time of the gunshots, and a bullet narrowly missed him. The bank worker's telephone call to the police allowed the officers to identify the shooter's location and arrest him.

On December 21, 1980, the hotel evacuated one hundred residents when smoke billowed across the eleventh floor. Two mattresses had caught fire in an empty bedroom. Chief Jim Young and his crew doused the flames, which had been confined to a single location. However, Cecil's management confirmed a damage estimate of $4,000.

On March 27, 1988, thousands watched Bono and U2 band perform a concert on the roof of a single-story liquor store at the corner of Sixth and Main Streets. The musicians parlayed the burgeoning notoriety of its next-door neighbor, the Cecil Hotel, as the backdrop for the band's latest music video, which featured the hit song "Where the Streets Have No Name."

Arrests, suicides and violence at the hotel continued throughout the decade. In 1988, police hauled twenty-eight-year-old Robert Sullivan from his hotel room for allegedly murdering his girlfriend, thirty-two-year-old Teri Frances Craig. The killing took place at the Huntington Beach home they had shared for the past seven years.

On September 1, 1992, the police discovered a body in the alley behind the hotel. Authorities believed the man either fell, jumped or had been pushed from the fifteenth floor. The victim stood about five feet, nine inches tall and weighed around 185 pounds. He wore blue sweatpants and a black sweatshirt over a gray T-shirt. The police guessed his age to be somewhere between twenty and thirty-two, but they failed to come up with an actual identity.

Problems that escaped major news coverage continually plagued the Cecil. In one case, police officer Larry Soeltz patiently talked down a drunken woman who threatened to jump from a tenth-floor window, saving her life. The papers rarely reported the hauling in of drunks, loiterers, prostitutes and nickel-and-dime drug dealers.

Each negative incident metastasized the hotel's cancerous reputation as it spread through the public sector, the hotel's residents and the civil authorities. The Coen Brothers patterned the rundown Hotel Earle on the Cecil in their 1991 black comedy film, *Barton Fink*. The postmodernist movie draws upon murder, violence and a fictional serial killer named Madman Mundt.

In 1995, fourteen inmates escaped from Pitchess Honor Rancho Jail in Castaic, California. The prisoners climbed over a razor wire fence by protecting their hands with socks. Once free, Eric Reed separated from the group, stripped to his underwear and convinced a driver that he had been robbed. The driver dropped him off at the Cecil Hotel, where the LAPD arrested the twenty-four-year-old, a felon who had smothered his infant son. The authorities returned Reed to Maine, where a jury convicted him of murder.

Punk rockers Blink-182 shot a video from the roof of the next-door building for their 2001 hit song, "The Rock Show," taken from the group's fourth album, *Take Off Your Pants and Jacket*. A crowd gathered as the band tossed dollar bills onto the street beneath them. A view of the Cecil Hotel sign appeared in the background throughout much of the song.

Incidents of violence continued throughout the first few decades of the twenty-first century. The *Los Angeles Times*, on July 8, 2003, reported that a maid cleaning rooms at the Cecil came upon the body of an unknown strangled man, but little else is known.

In May 2010, another odd occurrence struck the media. Ten-year fire department paramedic veteran Charles Anthony MacDougall advised his partner at the first-floor Cecil coffee shop that he needed to go upstairs to examine a resident. After about eight minutes, MacDougall's partner took the staircase to check on his coworker. He found him bleeding from knife wounds to the elbow and body.

Until the date of the stabbing, MacDougall had earned a sterling reputation, and the department had pegged him for the Paramedic of the Year Award. However, under questioning, the examiners discovered numerous inconsistencies in his explanation of the circumstances regarding how and why he received the wounds. The true cause of the fracas remained questionable. The police declined to press charges against MacDougall, but the department placed him on temporary administrative leave.

On June 15, 2015, the police removed the body of a deceased, unknown twenty-eight-year-old male from the Main Street sidewalk due to an apparent suicide or murder. The Cecil's assistant manager confirmed the deceased had not been a guest and may have been an intruder.

Over the years, the Cecil witnessed at least sixteen known suicides, dozens of violent acts, untold drug deals and countless arrests. The police visited its lobby on a consistent basis. Those blithely walking through the hotel's doors unknowingly stepped into a rhumba of rattlesnakes. Amy Price, the hotel manager between 2010 and the hotel's closing on January 1, 2017, estimated some eighty natural and unnatural deaths during her tenure.

Strange and inexplicable events, including murder, self-destruction and criminal activity, have plagued the Cecil for nearly a century. One can readily understand why thirty-year-resident Michael Sadowe referred to his home as "Hotel Suicide."

9

THE REST OF THE STORY

Many have tried to help the Skid Row area. However, a "great wall" separated the various groups of benefactors. One side pushed for humanitarian assistance to the poor as a top priority. The other emphasized the upgrade of blighted buildings to gentrify the corridor. While each championed competing solutions to improve downtown, the homeless remained as unfortunate pawns in their political machinations.

Skid Row's abject poverty and the required social services needed to support the underserved stymied the incentive for investment in physical improvements; 40 percent of Skid Row's population fell beneath the poverty level. Overburdened hospitals and psychiatric health facilities routinely dumped their overflow into the neighborhood like so much garbage. Many of the area's residents suffered from post-traumatic stress disorder (PTSD), schizophrenia, depression or other mental and physical ills. Others sported extensive criminal records. Up to ten thousand homeless souls lived on the streets within a four-mile radius of the Cecil Hotel. The city unofficially followed a policy of containment, maintaining Skid Row as a holding pen for the damaged and deranged. Nighttime brought out tent city for the homeless.

The Cecil had changed hands several times over the years, primarily due to financial weakness. Property tax records showed that the Angel Lopez Family Trust had purchased the hotel on April 15, 1984, from the Jack Lerner and Josefa Trust. On April 7, 1998, Streetwise Investments LLC purchased the hotel from Universal Foreclosure Services—evidence of the

Homeless civil rights activist Ted Hayes among Skid Row's tents. *Image from Wikimedia Commons.*

Cecil's struggles during the last decade of the twentieth century and the early years of the twenty-first century.

In 2006, police chief William Britton instituted the "broken windows" program in high-crime locales like Skid Row, with the policy of issuing tickets for minor offenses to the homeless for innocuous crimes like loitering, littering, prostitution and begging. Britton argued that small infractions led to serious crimes, and he intended to clean up the area. Other officials had applied strong-arm methods in the past. In June 1947, LAPD chief Clemenceau B. Horrall ordered a "blockade raid," rounding up 350 homeless individuals. Horrall announced a virtual elimination of crime during the following week.

To counter Britton's hard-nosed policy, city council approved the Jones Agreement on October 15, 2007. The program decriminalized sleeping on the streets until the area provided adequate accommodations for the homeless. Although the Cecil contained small rooms, provided minimal service, housed drug dealers and had a history of suicides, killings, killers and even foul water, the hotel provided a definite upgrade to a night on the streets.

Skid Row sign.
*Courtesy of the Library
of Congress.*

As the area around Skid Row declined, the Cecil's ability to survive plummeted. Lawsuits, physical deterioration of the building, tenant vacancies, reduced cash flow, an adverse political environment and a questionable location squeezed the hotel's ability to repay its lenders.

The elegant lobby served as a holding tank for transients and ne'er-do-wells. Only the lowest echelon of the Cecil's tenants accepted rooms without bathrooms. Caught up in the never-never land of $40 to $50 nightly and $470 monthly maximum rates, the hotel floundered in a turbulent sea of debt. The owners floated desperate ideas to save the drowning hulk.

On May 25, 2007, an organization called the 640 South Main Street Partners bought out the Streetwise Investments group. The new developers suggested a conversion of the Cecil into a budget-friendly spot called the Pearl. A small influx of credit permitted a lobby renovation, new outfits for security workers and a coat of paint on the downstairs walls. However, reality struck when guests entered the miserably appointed upper rooms. Drug dealers and lowlifes still roamed the halls.

Tenant Suzanne Bernal, age forty-five, complained to the *Los Angeles Times* about the possibility of being dispossessed if the hotel converted to more upscale suites. To protect victims like Bernal against homelessness, city council banned the demolition of 240 so-called flophouses and slowed the Cecil's plans. Los Angeles's battle to balance the need for downtown affordable housing for the homeless with the removal of urban blight continued.

Renovations at the Cecil halted when the city informed the owners of a new ordinance mandating that residential hotels must find temporary locations for their residents while buildings were converted from residential to standard use. The Cecil assumed the ordinance did not apply to it. The city disagreed, and a lawsuit ensued.

In 2008, prior to the recession, experienced "value-added," business-savvy Fred B. Cordova III, a Harvard MBA graduate, entered the picture to broker the sale of the hotel. Downtown was experiencing a renaissance with the recent opening of such facilities as the Walt Disney Concert Hall. The timing seemed ideal. The LAPD assisted by pushing the homeless out of the Main Street and Fifth Street corridor and deeper into Skid Row.

The goal called for the remodeling of the Cecil into a more modern "with-it" spot that appealed to young professionals. Cordova intended to upgrade the tenants' lifestyle experience and correspondingly increase the property's value. To put it another way, he intended to bring a zombie location like the Cecil back to the land of the living. The *Los Angeles Times* referred to the hotel's potential as a place where "the hip and the nearly homeless meet."[50]

Cordova eventually joined a group purchasing the Cecil for $26.5 million. He intended to rebrand the property as a mecca for the younger set. In opposition to his plan, the city declared a moratorium on the conversion of low-income housing to market rates. Relying on a loophole to overcome the statute, the owners created a new hotel called Stay on Main with the same address as the Cecil but a separate entrance and a coffee shop called Marty. The fulfillment of a proposed $7 million renovation remained on hold due to the city's measures, preventing the conversion of low-income housing units to market-rate residences.

The successful settlement of a lawsuit in January 2012 opened the door for the building to convert to 301 residential units and 299 hotel rooms. The agreement also resolved a counterclaim filed by former residents and the Los Angeles Community Action Network charging rent control violations. According to attorney Barbara Schultz, the hotel satisfied the suit with a $90,000 payment.

"The settlement generally established the Cecil as a residential hotel and established damage for some long-term tenants who had been illegally moved and relocated," explained Becky Dennison of the Community Action Network.[51]

Cordova wrote to city council in early 2012 to justify the new policies he had established:

> *When we took over the Cecil, it was in crisis. The previous operators turned a blind eye to what was going on inside with their guests. Drug dealers would check in and set up shop, and customers would come in, rent a room*

and spend the next several days getting high. Police reports reflected an average of more than a death a month and in some months as many as six from overdoses and drug-related matters. Since we "cleaned" up the hotel, the incidents of such have practically disappeared. Many lives have been saved! The Cecil is no longer a safe haven for criminals to prey on the less fortunate in our society.[52]

The renovation and personnel changes drastically reduced police calls to the Cecil. LAPD sergeant Michael Flanagan had difficulty recalling a single case of prostitution under the new owners.

Regardless of the so-called improvements, the Los Angeles Housing Department penalized the Cecil for a series of building code violations under the city's Rent Escrow Account Program (REAP), which the hotel management derogatorily called RAPE. Hotel officials appealed the ruling that allowed tenants to pay discounted rents, with money placed in escrow until the owners cured the defects. Cordova discovered renovating a property proved to be a long and difficult process in Los Angeles.

Cordova left the partnership in 2012, due to the financial and political challenges he encountered. Herb Chase III, a Lewis and Clark graduate and partner in the company Multi-Housing Capital Advisors Inc., took over the lead role. Principals Chase, Peter Sherman and Curtis Palmer previously had completed more than $20 billion in sales and financing transactions and possessed extensive experience with underperforming properties.

According to a March 15 letter to the hotel's residents, a dozen construction and heating issues required attention. Chase, as managing partner of the Main Street property, advised that permits had been pulled to update the electrical system for the eighty-five-year-old heating system. He anticipated completion of the repairs within ten weeks. He complained to REAP that previous owners had removed walls without proper authorization and that the new owners should not be held responsible. Chase contacted the Housing Authority to reconsider and repeal its decision.

The Cecil Hotel remained bogged down in a swamp of controversy and bureaucracy. A group called Home for the Good pushed for the Cecil's upgrade. Receiving support from the Department of Human Services, the Chamber of Commerce and the United Way, the Cecil proposed a compromise. It suggested making 384 apartments for the homeless and underserved along with an appropriate suite of social services. The building would operate as a mix of budget hotel rooms and low-income housing. In addition, they planned to add 75 affordable and 75 market-rate apartments, each measuring 165 square feet. To enhance the lower floors, plans called for a mix of new retail stores and a restaurant. The group drew up a comprehensive twenty-page proposal for the building, complete with maps, floor plans and color renderings.

Chase's Cecil Main Street Management LLC, which took over on March 26, 2012, proposed an investment of $10 million into the Cecil, which he viewed as a win-win prospect for the homeless, the company and the city. His investors would own an up-to-date property, the low-income residents would have a truly wonderful spot to live and the city would obtain a higher tax base.

Many members of the downtown retail community opposed the project, pointing to the availability of three thousand low-income rooms. The Rosslyn, the New Pershing and the Gateway Apartments stood among the dozens of properties available to the homeless.

Tom Gilmore, the developer of the Old Bank District Housing, spoke in opposition to the Cecil request: "The concept of so many new supportive units in one building is questionable as a policy, but to add them to an already stressed neighborhood is unconscionable."[53]

County Supervisor Gloria Molina summed up her own kibosh: "Good project, wrong place." The Historic Preservation Commission objected to the containment of the homeless to one area. At a February 13, 2014 meeting, Chase's proposal unraveled. Jerry Neuman, a cochair for the Home for the Good, threw in the sponge. "At the end of the day, we heard from the community.…Neither the county nor Home for the Good wanted to impose a project upon a neighborhood that wasn't prepared for it. Additionally, the requisite political support was not there."[54]

Chase returned to the drawing board. As money dried up with an adverse economy, management nixed its investment plans, The owners oscillated between the viability of a yuppie refuge and an asylum for the destitute.

With his alternatives limited by government realities, Chase negotiated with the CBRE group (Caldwell Banker Richard Ellis), the world's largest real estate company. On February 13, 2013, various media announced that Chase's Multi-Housing Capital group had become a part of the CBRE network, enhancing his clout. Ironically, that press release was published within a day of the discovery of Elisa Lam's body in the Cecil's water cistern.

Without improvements, the Cecil's reputation continued its nosedive. A longtime resident named Sally described maids turning tricks, drug overdoses and the extortion of residents by hotel workers. Employees confirmed the ugly secrets most hotels hide. Tasheyla MacClean, a former assistant manager, advised that the hotel basement held bloody mattresses sheathed in black plastic taken from rooms where suicides or murders had taken place. She also confirmed that the public greatly underestimated the death count at the hotel.

An online Yelp review compared the Cecil to a scary *Saw* movie. Sherry T. of Elsinore, California, wrote a one-star review: "This place is extremely haunted....We saw a ghost. It was a lady."

Kristen L. of Lexington Park, Maryland, penned a one-star review on May 31, 2018:

> *As others have said, the beautiful lobby is just a fantastic illusion. Once I stepped on the elevator, I knew I was in trouble. I was alone with my two-year old. We stepped into a hallway that made me think we were stepping back into time...paint peeling...tiles all jacked up. Shared bathroom that was nasty. And the room—I walked into a bed and a sink. The bedding had holes and stains. There was no AC in the midst of July. I cracked the window to get some kind of air and heard the lovely strains of a woman screaming down on the street. It takes a lot to freak me out, but this place did me in. And I did not know the history of this hotel nor ever heard of it until I stayed there.*

Phillip W. of Los Angeles wrote on February 2, 2013:

> *Honestly, we stayed in the hotel, not in spite of, but because of recent news. It has a rich history of suicide, violent crime and now a mysterious water-tank death, so thought it would be a thrill-seeking expedition. The real horror in this hotel is the treatment of guests. Far overpriced for the furnitureless crap hole that each room is. I feel like the whole business model is set up to take advantage of tourists who don't know better. The "premium queen room," despite being totally barren, was coated in some allergenic dust that made it difficult to sleep. The door to the room was damaged, appearing as if some previous attempts to kick it in had been made. At no point in a guest's stay would it ever be possible to obtain any level of comfort in these tiny rooms. What cements my one-star rating is the behavior of the employees. We were respectful and polite through the whole stay, but were treated like a burden to the establishment....In conclusion, spend the money on a real hotel. I don't know what you've done where you think you deserve a tiny, barren room with an unfriendly staff and noisy awful surroundings, but it's time to forgive yourself and stay at the Doubletree, or just sleep under a bridge or something.*

Dan'a R. of Los Angeles wrote on December 23, 2014: "Not in a good area, period! Do not be fooled into thinking this place is closed. It is now called Stay on Main. Until security is stepped up in this place, I would not suggest it to anyone. This is not an area where you even want to stay. No tourist attractions and loads of sketchy areas nearby. It also has a very unsavory past."

The Bedbug Registry listed eleven complaints. John L. wrote on February 17, 2015: "Yes, indeed, bugs are a major problem at the Cecil." Itchy Queen wrote on June 20, 2012: "Today, I woke up itchy, and the first thing that popped up in my head was bedbugs. I looked all over my body and found nine bites."

Other patrons complained of hair in the shower and dirt in the bed, smudge marks on the headboard and a television not working. Comments like, "You get what you pay for," and, "The clientele is nothing to write home about," abound on TripAdvisor. User ratings on Expedia listed 2.2 stars out of a possible five rating. Yelp provided an even lower 1.5 star rating, with one reviewer stating, "The Cecil is where dreams go to die."

When an English couple started to walk toward the entertainment area after dark, a doorman stopped them. "I strongly suggest you take a taxi. It is far better for your health if you take my advice"

Although most of the Yelp ratings proved negative, a few adventurous souls provided positive comments. Wendy S. of Lebanon, Oregon, gave the Cecil a sterling four-star rating on March 26, 2016: "I lived here for a month in the 80s. It was eighty-five dollars per week. My neighbor across the hall sold drugs but was a super nice guy. There was a Chinese restaurant downstairs and a bakery next door....I was young with a small child, and I found it a cool experience. It's in a super location. I'd love to go back!"

Visitor F. of Culver City, California, gave the Cecil a five-star review on July 19, 2020: "We need this place to reopen!!! It's a beautiful, historical place, and the creepiness of it makes it even more worth it. If you love the architecture and the stories, rate it a good five stars."

Paranormalists considered the Cecil Hotel one of the world's most haunted locations. In 2014, a young boy who loved scary stories, Koston Alderete, photographed a ghost-like specter dangling outside the window of room 451 of the hotel—supposed proof of the hotel's spiritual possession.

Despite all the negatives, Dr. Richard Born, whose company, BD Hotels, controlled an upscale portfolio of boutique hotels, paid $30 million to purchase the hotel under the name 248 Haynes Hotel Associates LLC on June 5, 2014. His group specialized in converting undervalued properties into hip lodgings for young professionals. Born controlled such New York gems as the Bowery, the Maritime, the Ludlow, the Blakely and the Greenwich. He believed his latest purchase, the Cecil, like his East Coast portfolio, possessed a wonderful "lack of fungibility" that made it unique and nearly impossible to replace.

In 2015, New York–based Simon Baron Development entered into a ninety-nine-year ground lease with Richard Born's company. Simon Baron intended to operate and renovate the hotel, its retail spaces and its residential entities. Highly respected University of Pennsylvania graduate and founder Jonathan Simon served as chairman, and Matthew Baron, a Columbia University graduate with an MBA, acted as president of Simon Baron. President Baron explained: "We plan to use this project as a catalyst to begin more projects on the West Coast, more specifically in the Los Angeles area."[55]

Baron bandied about a renovation investment of as much as $100 million in the Cecil. The Simon Baron–owned design firm Stage 3 Properties began to draw up the overall plans for the Cecil upgrade to a combination hotel/apartment facility.

To handle the details and oversee the product, Simon Baron brought in co-living specialist Ollie, a subsidiary of Stage 3. Ollie laid out the furnishings and the room layouts for the 301 fully furnished micro units. The tight 165 square feet of apartment living area combined dozens of features guaranteed to appeal to the upwardly mobile, single target audience—all at reasonable rents.

Every unit contained a couch that converted into a bed. To appeal to the younger professionals, their amenities included free WiFi, smart television programming, community social and educational programs, bike parking, weekly maid service, private bathrooms and keyless entry. When completed, the developers intended the Cecil to become the largest co-living community on the West Coast. Although the apartments failed to include a kitchen due to space considerations, the plan provided a food preparation area.

The developers set aside thirty thousand square feet of space for shared amenities, including a full gym and a rooftop wading pool. Management lined up the prestigious architectural firm of Omgivning, designers of dozens of mixed-use projects, including the Broadway, the Proper Hotel and the Hellman, to draw up the blueprints and design the open spaces. Best of all, Ollie estimated monthly rents at about $1,500 per month, a highly competitive rate for downtown Los Angeles.

Chris Bledsoe, cofounder of Stage 3's co-living division, believed young professionals would gladly exchange living space for reasonable rental rates and a lifestyle fitting their needs. In addition, the layout and furnishings had been blocked out to make 165 square feet feel more like double that amount.

President Matthew M. Baron announced, "We are going to redevelop it from the doorway to the roof and everything in between." The Stay on Main's hotel rooms were then rented for about $50 per night, but Baron aimed to create a boutique hotel that would compete with other popular hotels, such as the Ace a few blocks away, whose daily room rates started at $199. Baron anticipated slightly lower prices for his project, perhaps $150 per night. "We really think it's a fantastic location—the center, where everything is happening."[56]

When questioned about overcoming the Cecil's unsavory past, Baron took a positive slant. He considered the hotel's eerie past an asset. Clients came because of, rather than despite, the murders and suicides involved.

"We sort of envisioned a market that would skew younger, around twenty-two to early thirties, maybe single, and don't need as much space and are cost-conscious," Matthew Baron explained.[57] He recognized that reduced sizes reduced the impact of the soaring construction costs, an important value factor.

Baron required approval from the Community Redevelopment Agency's governing board (CRA/LA) to get the necessary permits before he could proceed. Rick Cocoa, a spokesman for Councilman Jose Huizar, who represented downtown, advised the media that complete plans had yet to be filed with the city.

In late 2014, a revamped Regent Theater reopened on Main Street, and the construction of the Holland luxury apartment began a few blocks away at the former location of the Union Rescue Mission. Developers scheduled an opening of two hotels near Broadway and Ninth Street near the Ace. The Broad Museum on Grand planned a 2015 start date. The surrounding activity convinced the Baron Group that the Cecil sat in a potentially trendy area with strong upward potential.

As the original plans morphed to meet regulatory and investment realities, Simon Baron's chief executive officer Steve Valenzuela specified that the program would include a low-income segment. The latest plan required the rehabbing and repurposing of 261 single-room residential units and the building of thirty new units at a nearby property already under lease no later than July 2028.

The city previously approved a reduction of single-room-occupancy (SRO) residential units from 301 to 291 to allow for ten manager units. The Skid Row Housing Trust would operate the SRO units, available to tenants making 30 to 60 percent of the area's median income. Many of the units, 141 of them, would be available to those making less than 30 percent of the area's median income. A covenant ensured that this section of the property would continue as affordable housing for fifty-five years.

The Stay on Main's elegant but faded lobby remained a symbol of its macabre past, like a dusty railroad depot that had seen better times. Management had added bright orange colors to floors four through six, added bunk beds and a new entryway, but the Band-Aid improvements could not stem its downward trend. The café remained closed; the entertainment room's large-screen television stood dark. Outside, the mixed neighborhood teemed with the homeless.

On January 1, 2017, General Manager Amy Price reported that the Cecil Hotel had closed its doors. Only a few permanent lodgers remained.

On Tuesday, February 28, 2017, by a ten-to-zero unanimous vote, the city council officially accepted the recommendations of the Planning and Land Use Management Committee and Cultural Heritage Commission, approving developer Matthew Baron's request to grant landmark status for the Cecil. The committee cited the structure's high level of integrity regarding its design and materials and the extent of its originality as positives.

In a city of fantastic wealth, the Skid Row area of Los Angeles held thousands of homeless but provided only nine public toilets. Several years earlier, the area contained twenty-seven Porta-Potty installations. Sidewalks required constant hosing to remove human feces and trash. Tuberculosis, hepatitis and other communicable diseases ran rampant. The local Veterans Hospital complained that homeless ex-servicemen with substance abuse stank of urine.

A 2013 United Nations report listed 14,000 arrests in the tougher areas of Los Angeles for the year. Sociologists compared the plight of the homeless in Skid Row to the experiences of citizens of third-world countries. A report for the four-month period from July to October 2019 listed a total of 997 crimes within a half-mile radius of Skid Row's center with a breakdown as follows: 27 percent larceny, 25 percent assault, 22 percent vehicle break in, 13 percent robbery, 6 percent burglary, 4 percent auto theft and 1 percent sex crimes. Figures for arson and homicide totaled a little over 1 percent. The estimated full-time homeless population of Skid Row in and around the Cecil for 2019 stood at 2,783, but the actual total stood much higher.

As early as November 2016, Mayor Eric Garcetti led a coalition to pass Proposition HHH, providing for a $1.2 billion bond to construct housing

The interior of the Cecil Hotel. *Image from the Historical-Cultural Monument application, City of Los Angeles.*

for up to ten thousand homeless in the city. Unfortunately, building progress traveled at a snail's pace.

By September 2019, only nine occupants remained at the almost empty Cecil. Management permitted those tenants to stay prior to the onset of construction. Then, they would be temporarily relocated until the project's completion.

The Cecil's plans changed again in 2020. The latest renderings for the interior renovation of the Cecil by Marmol Radziner aimed for a bright, white lobby. The Los Angeles–based firm with San Francisco and New York offices presented designs to the city's cultural commission that returned many key external and internal features to their 1924 original form while modernizing color schemes and overall appearances.

John LoCasio of the Historic Resources Group acted as a consultant for the developers of the heavily delayed project. "'Non-historic storefronts along Main Street will be removed, along with some of the hotel's signs and its marquee. New storefronts made to match the original façades will be installed instead. The hotel's blade signs and the large painted wall sign on the building's south face are set to be restored and new entrance doors to the hotel will be installed. The lobby's interior elements will be retained,' LoCasio said, 'though the marble flooring and finishes will be replaced with terrazzo.'"[58]

Residents of the 264 units operated by the Skid Row Housing Trust would enter by a separate elevator and entrance. Floors two through seven, plus half of the eighth floor, would accommodate low-income residents. The remaining 299 rooms on the upper floors would be used for a hotel.

An article on Curbed by Bianca Barragan indicated the Cecil could reopen just around the corner in 2021. Adding veracity to Barragan's story, a December 2020 article confirmed that the Slate Property Group and Atalaya Capital Management partnered to provide a $30 million mezzanine loan to reposition the former Cecil into multifamily and boutique hotel use. "The financing along with a $15,000,000 senior loan from Centennial Bank will generate the funds to upgrade and modernize the Cecil…and to create an uptick in investment in hospitality and hotel development in Southern California."[59]

On April 3, 2021, Matthew Baron updated the LADT News, "We have no intention right now of reopening the hotel. Originally, we were going to rebuild the whole thing and build a hotel with apartments.…It's tough to build a hotel during COVID. There are a lot more difficult things going on in the world than that decision…but for now, it's tabled. There's some repair work going on at the building, and it still houses some long-time tenants with protection from the city, but there's really nothing happening now."[60]

As we come to the end of the story, the Cecil continues to generate news. Ryan Murphy's *American Horror Story*'s fifth season on FX took place at the Cortez Hotel, a thinly veiled copy of the Cecil. In the episode "The Devil's Night," Cecil's own Richard Ramirez joined serial killers Jeffrey Dahmer, John Wayne Gacy and the Zodiac Killer for dinner. Adventurous fans dribbled into to the real hotel, renamed the Stay on Main, to stay in the city's, and perhaps the country's, scariest hotel until its closure.

The Cecil remained an active stop on Esotouric's four-hour Hotel Horrors and Main Street Vice Bus Tour, which ran between the hours of noon and 4:00 p.m.

The Discovery Plus channel aired a January 4, 2021 show featuring the Cecil on *Ghost Adventures*. The episode filmed the glow of evil that surrounded the rooms once inhabited by Richard Ramirez, Jack Unterweger and the unknown killer of Goldie Osgood. The host implored Elisa Lam to reveal her mystery. Each room visited chilled the investigatory team.

Netflix presented a four-part saga on Richard Ramirez, and Netflix premiered a Cecil documentary on February 10, 2021. The myth and history of the Cecil continues to fascinate the public.

In a publicity stunt, Lydia Dupra of Heaux Cosmetics paid $500 to a security guard for two bottles of water from the hotel. "I purchased the water because I saw value in the opportunity. As of right now, I own the only specimens in the world, one bottle from Richard Ramirez's room 1419 and one from Elisa Lam's room 506."[61] Dupra posted a video of the exchange on TikTok and garnered two hundred thousand viewers in less than a month. The hotel promptly fired the guard. Although Dupra received the touch of celebrity status she craved, she experienced anxiety and insomnia since taking the water home. In addition, several online viewers have criticized her insensitivity.

With the COVID epidemic stifling the tourism industry, the hospitality sector, convention centers, restaurants and hotels through 2020, 2021 and into 2022, the Cecil's struggle to balance its nonexistent revenue with costs remained tantamount. Almost one-fifth of securitized hotel loans had fallen thirty days or more past due during 2021.

The City of Los Angeles instituted Project Roomkey, a collaborative effort with the county, state and Homeless Services Authority (LAHSA) to secure hotel rooms for the disadvantaged during the COVID-19 outbreak. Whether the Cecil took part in the program remains uncertain.

City financial records listed the Cecil's 2020 assessed value at $32,472,963, its 2019 city taxes at $401,917 and its mortgage incumbrance at $14,400,000.

FINAL UPDATE FROM THE AUTHOR

On Sunday, November 27, 2021, the author visited the Cecil shortly before dark. The locked and shuttered doors blocked my chance to enter the building. Passersby nosed around the front entrance, naturally curious about the infamous hotel. Several snapped pictures on their iPhones as they whispered to one another about serial killer Richard Ramirez, pointed to the upper floors where jumpers had leaped to their deaths or questioned the mysterious death of Elisa Lam.

The area surrounding the hotel appeared desolate, a war zone of emptiness, with plenty of "For Rent" signs attached to the unoccupied buildings. Just a few blocks away, Skid Row stood as a vast wasteland, with tent city housing the homeless, a most unsafe and unsavory place to be after dark. My Uber driver, a woman, appeared especially uneasy as I snapped a few pictures and poked around the exterior of the building.

Obvious deterioration of the Cecil seized my eye. Unappetizing sheets of brown paper covered the front windows to block inside visibility. Four individual signs spaced around the windows read: "Now Leasing! Accepting Vouchers and Section 8." The signs also pictured interior photos of renovated Cecil rooms "in the heart of the city." Two other signs warned, "Private Property," in bold red print. A smaller sign stated: "For any delivery into the building, please call 424-206-3994." Like the crossbones on a bottle of iodine, the overall appearance signaled danger, but it appeared work might be progressing inside the building during the week.

A coat of paint covered up the Cecil's original signage on the side of the building promoting its low rates. However, another high rise around the corner retained its painted Cecil business sign on its upper wall. A red advertisement promoting "Homemade Hamburgers" stood at the base of the left-hand alley wall, but graffiti swarmed around it with a vengeance. The Cecil appeared sad and lonely.

Scuttlebutt hinted at a Cecil reopening in some form or another. Local boosters hoped a coat of paint, assorted upgrades, a change of ownership and a restructuring of the rooms would overcome almost one hundred years of deaths, suicides and unfortunate endings.

COVID had changed everything. In December 2021, just a month after my visit, following four years of inactivity, the Cecil rose from the ashes like the proverbial Phoenix. Reporter Bianca Barragan announced that the Cecil Hotel had quietly reopened as an affordable housing project. Developer Matthew Baron told the press, "Once COVID hit, the feasibility of new

Photographs by Michele Perelman.

hotel projects went away....Our business plan was taken by the pandemic, but once that happened, we looked at what the best thing we could do with the building was."[62]

Baron recognized the futility of opening a downtown Los Angeles hotel. Occupancy rates stood at less than 50 percent during the third quarter of 2021, according to a report from the Downtown Center Business District

Opposite: *Photograph by Michele Perelman.*

Right: The Cecil Hotel's front entrance, 2021. *Courtesy of Cody Danker.*

(it was actually 48.7 percent, a significant improvement over the dismal 39.6 percent of a year ago, but nowhere near the pre-pandemic level of 80 percent).

Baron coordinated with the Skid Row Housing Trust to convert the Cecil into low-rent housing and obtain the proper approvals. The unique features of the property and the fact that it required rehabbing rather than new construction enhanced the ease and practicality of completion. Baron estimated an overall cost of $75 million.

At its grand opening, the Cecil management announced its ability to provide six hundred single-person, efficiency rooms, ranging from 160 to 176 square feet in size. Residents would be required to earn between 30 and 60 percent of the area's median income in order to be eligible for a rental, with the majority of the spots geared to the lower end of the spectrum. A prior covenant required the Cecil to maintain below-market rates for a fifty-five-year period.

"Community amenities at the Cecil included a shared kitchen, secured entry and laundry facilities." Skid Row Housing Trust would manage the facility and provide the necessary health and human services assistance.

Many questions still remain. Will the Cecil's latest change to all low-income housing reduce its affinity for misfortune and calamity? Will the residents find peace in their new location? Hopefully, yes, but we shall see. We shall see.[63]

TIMELINE

December 20, 1924: Grand opening of the seven-hundred-room Cecil Hotel.

January 22, 1927: Percy Ormond Cook shoots himself.

November 19, 1931: W.K. Norton dies after ingesting poison.

September 1932: A maid discovers Benjamin Dodich, dead from a self-inflicted gunshot wound.

July 1934: Louis D. Borden is found in his room with his throat slashed.

March 1937: Grace E. Magro falls from the ninth floor to her death.

January 1938: Roy Thompson jumps from the top floor.

May 1939: Navy officer Erwin C. Neblett dies from self-inflicted poisoning.

January 1940: Teacher Dorothy Steiger ingests poison.

1941: The Albert family takes over ownership of the hotel.

September 1944: Dorothy Jean Purcell throws her just-delivered baby out the window.

January 14, 1947: The death of Elizabeth Short, the Black Dahlia

November 1947: Robert Smith jumps from the seventh floor to his death.

1950: Junior Realty takes control of the Cecil.

October 22, 1954: Helen Gurnee leaps from the seventh floor to her death.

1962: Julia Moore jumps from the seventh-floor window.

February 11, 1962: Pauline Otton jumps from the ninth floor, killing herself and pedestrian George Giannini.

June 4, 1964: A hotel worker discovers the body of "Pigeon Goldie" Osgood, who had been raped, robbed and murdered. The case remains unsolved.

December 11, 1974: Margret Schafer is murdered in Vienna by Jack Unterweger.

December 20, 1975: A woman registered as Allison Lowell jumps from the twelfth floor.

December 2, 1976: Jeffrey Thomas Palley is arrested after firing fifteen shots from the Cecil's roof.

April 15, 1984: The Angel Lopez Family Trust purchases the hotel from the Jack Lerner and Josefa Trust.

June 27,1984: Seventy-nine-year-old Jennie Vincow is murdered by Richard Ramirez.

March 17, 1985: Dayle Okazaki and Veronica Yu are murdered by Richard Ramirez.

March 26, 1985: Vincent and Maxine Zazzara are murdered by Richard Ramirez.

April 14, 1985: Bill Doi is murdered by Richard Ramirez.

May 29, 1985: Richard Ramirez rapes Nettie Lang and assaults Mabel Bell.

July 2, 1985: Mary Louise Cannon is murdered by Richard Ramirez.

July 4, 1985: Whitney Bennett survives a beating with a tire iron by Richard Ramirez.

July 7, 1985: Joyce Nelson is raped, robbed and murdered by Richard Ramirez.

July 8, 1985: Sophie Dickman is raped and robbed by Richard Ramirez.

July 20, 1985: Max and Leda Kneiding are murdered by Richard Ramirez.

July 21, 1985: Chainarong Khovananth is murdered by Richard Ramirez.

July 23, 1985: Virginia and Chris Peterson are shot by Richard Ramirez but survive.

August 8, 1985: Elyas Abowath is murdered by Richard Ramirez.

August 18, 1985: Peter and Barbara Pan are murdered by Richard Ramirez.

August 25, 1985: Bill Carns is murdered by Richard Ramirez.

August 31, 1985: Richard Ramirez, the "Night Stalker," is arrested.

April 7, 1988: Streetwise Investments LLC purchases the Cecil from Universal Foreclosure Services.

1988: Robert Sullivan is arrested at the Cecil for murder.

May 23, 1990: Jack Unterweger is released from jail after serving a fifteen-year sentence.

September 15, 1990: Blanka Bočková is murdered by Unterweger in Prague.

December 5, 1990: Heidemarie Hammerer is murdered by Unterweger near Bregenz.

October 26, 1990: Brunhilde Masser is murdered by Unterweger near Graz.

March 7, 1991: Elfriede Schrempf is murdered by Unterweger near Graz.

April 8, 1991: Silvia Zagler is murdered by Unterweger in the Vienna Woods.

April 16, 1991: Sabine Moitzi is murdered by Unterweger in Vienna Woods.

April 28, 1991: Regina Prem is murdered by Unterweger in Vienna Woods.

May 7, 1991: Karin Eroglu-Sladky is murdered by Unterweger in Vienna Woods.

June 19, 1991: Shannon Exley is murdered by Unterweger in Los Angeles.

June 28, 1991: Irene Rodriguez is murdered by Unterweger in Los Angeles.

July 3, 1991: Peggy Booth is murdered by Unterweger in Los Angeles.

September 1, 1992: An unknown Black man is pushed or jumps from the top floor.

February 27, 1992: Jack Unterweger is arrested in Miami.

2008: Fred Cordova is involved in the purchase of the Cecil.

2012: Multi-Housing Capital Advisors takes over from Fred Cordova.

February 13, 2013: Multi-Housing becomes part of the CBRE group.

February 19, 2013: Elisa Lam's body is discovered in the hotel's water tower.

2014: BD Hotels pays $30,000,000 for the Cecil.

June 13, 2015: The body of an unidentified male—possible suicide—is found.

2015: Simon Baron Development enters into a ninety-nine-year lease with BD Hotels.

December 2021: Cecil Hotel reopens as affordable housing.

NOTES

Chapter 1

1. Loy Lester Smith (1885–1956), a highly respected architect and Pomona College graduate, completed the plans for the twelve-story, eighty-four-thousand-square-foot Lane Mortgage Building, which opened in 1923, and the City Club, built two years later. Contractor Weymouth Crowell (1864–1952), a Canadian by birth, oversaw the construction and later worked on the Harold Lloyd House in Beverly Hills.

Chapter 2

2. Skid Row's name is derived from the term "skid road" in the Pacific Northwest, the path that allowed timber workers to skid logs. It came to denote an impoverished area where inhabitants are on the "skids."
3. Meares, "Suicide," KCET.

Chapter 3

4. Steve Hodel, February 27, 2019.
5. Elroy, *Black Dahlia*, 227.
6. Steve Hodel, February 27, 2019.
7. Nelson and Hudson, *Exquisite Corpse*, 18.
8. Haugen, *Shattered Dreams*, 69.
9. University of North Carolina, "Ed Burns."
10. Nelson and Hudson, *Exquisite Corpse*, 27.
11. Ibid., 44.

12. Wikipedia, "George Hodel."
13. Ibid.
14. Louise Springer was garroted to death on June 13, 1949, just two blocks from where Elizabeth Short's body had been found. Police believed the two murders were connected.

Chapter 4

15. Peter Kürten (1883–1931) was a German serial killer known as the "Vampire of Düsseldorf." He committed a series of horrific murders and crimes, for which the justice system sentenced him to the guillotine.
16. Wikipedia, "Skid Row Stabber," www.en.wikipedia.org.

Chapter 5

17. Anton Szandor LaVey (1930–1997) founded the Church of Satan in 1966 and penned numerous books on Satanism.
18. Carlo, *Night Stalker*, 26.
19. Ibid., 29.
20. Ibid., 50.
21. Ibid., 71.
22. Ibid., 76.
23. Ibid., 108.
24. Ibid., 140.
25. Ibid., 162–63.
26. Ibid., 256.
27. Miller, "Penn Exchanged Notes."
28. Carlo, *Night Stalker*, 517–18.

Chapter 6

29. Leake, *Entering Hades*, chap. 9, loc. 881.
30. Alexander, *Johann "Jack" Unterweger*, loc. 22.
31. Hamilton, "Killer Who Crossed Continents."
32. Jean Genet (the son of a prostitute) served prison time for thievery and homosexuality. Once freed from prison, he gained fame as a French novelist, playwright, poet, essayist and political activist. He remained a free man throughout his life. Norman Mailer was a two-time Pulitzer Prize–winning author, with such hit novels as *The Naked and the Dead* and *The Executioner's Song*.
33. Leake, *Entering Hades*, chap. 3, loc. 189.
34. Graz is Austria's second-largest city, with a population exceeding 283,000, and Bregenz is a small city on the western edge of the country.
35. Leake, *Entering Hades*, chap. 5, loc. 722.

36. Alexander, *Johann "Jack" Unterweger*, loc. 186.
37. Ibid.

Chapter 7

38. Anderson, *Gone at Midnight*, 62.
39. Ibid., 57.
40. Ibid., 135.
41. Ibid., 199.
42. Ibid., 28.
43. Ibid., 233.
44. Ibid., 242.
45. Ibid., 73.
46. Ibid., 171.
47. Rylah, "Hotel Employee."
48. Anderson, *Gone at Midnight*, 296.

Chapter 8

49. One report listed Goldie Osgood's age as sixty-five instead of seventy-nine.

Chapter 9

50. Guzman, "Shake-Up."
51. Anderson, *Gone at Midnight*, 256–57.
52. Evans, "Strange Saga."
53. Ibid.
54. Hotel Business, "Baron Development."
55. Khouri, "Once a Den of Prostitution and Drugs."
56. Boerner, "Smaller Apartments."
57. Ibid.
58. Barragan, "First Glimpse."
59. Cornfield, "Slate Property."
60. Donahue, "No Opening Date."
61. Fowler, "Fan Collects Tap Water."
62. Barragan, "Hotel Reopens."
63. Although the hotel may be referred to as Hotel Cecil, the Cecil or the Cecil Hotel, I have opted to call it the Cecil or the Cecil Hotel to maintain consistency throughout this book.

BIBLIOGRAPHY

Books

Alexander, Andrew. *Johann "Jack" Unterweger: International Serial Killer.* True Crime Books. Kindle Edition, 2019.

Anderson, Jake. *Gone at Midnight: The Mysterious Death of Elisa Lam.* New York: Citadel Press, 2020.

Becker, Shawn. *Criminal Psychology: The Criminal Mind of a Serial Killer.* Self-published. United Kingdom, 2016.

Carlo, Philip. *The Night Stalker: The Life and Crimes of Richard Ramirez.* New York: Pinnacle Books, 1996.

Eatwell, Piu Marie. *Black Dahlia, Red Rose: The Crime, Corruption and Coverup of America's Greatest Unsolved Murder.* New York: Liveright, 2017.

Farrell, John. *Ben Weingart & the Weingart Foundation.* Los Angeles, CA: Weingart Foundation, 2002.

Gilmore, John. *Severed: The True Story of the Black Dahlia Murder.* Los Angeles, CA: Amok Books, 2006.

Gladwell, Malcolm. *Talking to Strangers.* New York: Little, Brown & Co., 2019.

Haugen, Brenda. *The Black Dahlia: Shattered Dreams.* Mankato, MN: Compass Point Books, 2010.

Hodel, Fauna. *One Day She'll Darken: The Mysterious Beginnings of Fauna Hodel.* Parker, CO: Outskirts Press, 2008.

Hodel, Steve. *Black Dahlia Avenger: A Genius for Murder—The True Story.* New York: Arcade Publishing, 2015.

Kaminsky, Michelle. *Serial Killer Trivia.* Berkeley, CA: Ulysses Press, 2019.

Leake, John. *Entering Hades: The Double Life of a Serial Killer.* New York: Sarah Crichton Books, 2007.

Nelson, Mark, and Sarah Hudson Bayliss. *Exquisite Corpse: Surrealism and the Black Dahlia Murder.* New York: Bullfinch Press, 1967.

Newton, Michael. *The Encyclopedia of Serial Killers*. New York: Checkmark Books, 2006.

Patios, Mary. *Childhood Shadows: The Hidden Story of the Black Dahlia Murder*. Bloomington, MN: Authorhouse, 2007.

Vronsky, Peter. *Serial Killers: The Methods and Madness of Monsters*. New York: Berkeley Books, 2004.

Woods, Damien. *Criminal Psychology: Understanding the Dark and Twisted Mind of a Serial Killer*. Self-published. United Kingdom, 2017.

Movies, Television, Podcasts and Audio

Berlinger, Joe, dir. *Crime Scene: The Vanishing at the Cecil Hotel*. Los Gatos, CA: Netflix, February 10, 2021.

Carrillo, Gil Lieutenant. "The Inside Story of the Night Stalker's Last Run." Posted on *LA Eastside* by Al Desmadre, August 27, 2010.

The Cecil Hotel's Dark History. CNN, February 22, 2013.

Coates, Carol, producer. *The Case of the Hillside Stranglers*. Los Angeles, CA: Metro-Golden-Mayer, April 2, 1989.

———. *Hillside Strangers*. Los Angeles, CA: Metro-Goldwyn-Mayer Studios, April 2, 1989.

Dark, Dark World Podcast. Episode 16, "Vaughn Greenwood: The Skid-Row Slasher." October 10, 2019.

Darker Side of Life Podcasts. "Elisa Lam." June 2, 2020.

DUH True Crime Podcast. "Black Dahlia." August 12, 2019.

Elroy, James. *The Black Dahlia*. New York: Penguin Random House Audiobooks, 2006.

FBI Files. Season 2, episode 14, "Killer Abroad." May 15, 1999.

Garcia, James Edward. *My Scary Diary*. "Cecil Hotel: Real Scary Moments." August 19, 2016. www.youtube.com.

Green, Bruce Seth, dir. *Manhunt: Search for the Night Stalker*. Westwood, CA: Leonard Hill Films, 1989.

Haunted Encounters. Season 1, episode 4, "Hotel Cecil." Paranormal TV, Bio. HD. December 22, 2012.

Horror Chronicles Podcast. "The Cecil Hotel." August 22, 2019.

Hot Pink Sun Podcast. "Staying at the Cecil Hotel." July 24, 2016. www.youtube.com.

Killer Jobs. Episode 27, "Jack Unterweger: The Vienna Strangler." February 19, 2019.

Lights Out. "Elisa Lam: The Haunted Cecil Hotel." May 15, 2020.

Mugshots: Kenneth Bianchi & Angelo Buono—The Hillside Stranglers. Parco Inc., True Crime Network, 2013.

Murderish. Episode 41, "Elisa Lam: Mysterious Death at Hotel Cecil." September 29, 2019.

Once Upon a Crime. "Infamous Locales: Chapter 3: The Cecil Hotel: Parts 1 and 2." May 28, 2018.

Palma, Brian, dir. *Black Dahlia.* New York: Universal Studios, 2006.

Russell, Tiller, dir. *The Night Stalker: Hunt for a Serial Killer.* Los Gatos, CA: Netflix, December 15, 2020.

Serial Killers. "The Vienna Strangler: Jack Unterweger." Parcast, January 9 and 16, 2019.

Simply Strange. Episode 29, "Cecil Hotel." November 27, 2019. www.youtube.com.

Sofa King Podcasts. Episode 333, "Richard Ramirez: The Night Stalker." February 26, 2018.

Very Scary People. "The Night Stalker." HLN. July 24, 2020.

Whistler, Simon, host. "The Cecil Hotel: The Deadliest Hotel in Los Angeles." Produced by Jennifer De Silva. GE Graphic Studios, January 29, 2020.

Newspapers and Magazines

Atkinson, Rick. "Killer Prose." *Washington Post,* August 3, 1994.

Bridge, Adrian. "Murderers Final Freedom: The Bizarre Life of Jack Unterweger, Poet and Killer of Prostitutes." *Independent,* July 3, 1994.

Conde Nast. "American Horror Story: Hotel Exists in Real Life." December 14, 2015. www.details.com.

Hangley, Bill, Jr., Andy Simmons and Marc Peyser. "They Got Away with Murder." *Readers Digest,* April 2020, 56–59.

Los Angeles Times. "Marital Strife Held Cause of Suicide Attempt." January 23, 1927.

———. "Mother Held After Baby Thrown to Death." September 8, 1944.

———. "Woman Takes Death Plunge." March 15, 1937.

Macfarlane, Robert. "A Murderous Talent." *New York Times,* January 13, 2008.

Malnic, Eric. "Bird Lover Slain, But Friends Remember." *Los Angeles Times,* June 6, 1964.

McGraw, Carol. "The Valley Intruder: William Doi, Monterey Park May 14." *Los Angeles Times,* August 25, 1985.

Melnick, Eric. "Austrian Slayer of L.A. Prostitutes Kills Self." *Los Angeles Times,* June 30, 1994.

Queally, James. "Bobby Joe Maxwell Dies at 69." *Los Angeles Times,* May 17, 2019.

Ramos, George, and Boris Yard. "Dead Man Is Identified as a Serial Killer of Ten." *Los Angeles Times,* February 6, 1987.

Sharon, Keith. "After Three Bullets in the Head, He Still Can't Escape the 'Night Stalker.'" *Orange County Register,* September 30, 2012.

Spokesman Review. "Slasher Jury Finds Man Guilty." December 30, 1976.

Zweig, Jason. "What History Tells Us About the Market." *Wall Street Journal,* October 8, 2008.

Internet

Anderson, Dave. "Top 10 Facts about Richard Ramirez the Night Stalker." ListLand. July 6, 2015. www.listland.com.

Barnes, Gene. "Mass Murderer Steve Nash." IWitness. 1957. www.iwitness.usc.edu.

Barragan, Bianca. "Downtowners Don't Want Scandalous Cecil Hotel Upgraded and Turned into Supportive Housing." Curbed LA. May 17, 2014. www.la.curbed.com.

———. "Downtown LA's Creepy Hotel Cecil Is Now a City Landmark." Curbed LA. March 2, 2017. www.la.curbed.com.

———. "First Glimpse: Marmol Radziner to Helm Hotel Cecil's Interior Renovations." Curbed LA. November 12, 2019. www.la.curbed.com.

———. "Hotel Cecil Could Finally Reopen in Late 2021." Curbed LA. September 3, 2019.

———. "Infamous Hotel Cecil Reopens as Affordable Housing Project, Hospitality Plans Scrapped as Coronavirus Casualty." Bisnow. December 15, 2021. www.bisnow.com.

———. "Inside the 100M Overhaul at Downtown's Cecil Hotel." Curbed LA. June 1, 2016. www.la.curbed.com.

Berman, Taylor. "Guests at L.A. Hotel Spent Weeks Drinking Water Contaminated by a Dead Body." *Gawker*, February 20, 2013. www.gawker.com.

Blaise, Amber. "Welcome to the Hotel California." Paranormal. August 29, 2020.

Boerner, Dean. "Smaller Apartments Are Doing Big Things for Developers." Bisnow. September 4, 2019. www.bisnow.com.

CBS News. "Questions Remain 3 Years After Woman's Body Was Found Inside L.A. Hotel's Rooftop Water Tank." October 31, 2016. www.cbsnews.com.

Chen, Cathaleen. "Co-Living Operator Ollie Is Unconcerned with Cecil's Haunted Past." TRD Los Angeles. September 20, 2016. www.therealdeal.com.

Cinema Libre Studio. "Lost Angels: Skid Row Is My Home." 2010. www.cinemalibrestudio.com.

Clark, Em. "Is the Cecil Still Open?" Soapboxie. August 31, 220. www.soapboxie.com.

Clarke, Katherine. "New York Developer Is Latest to Buy into DTLA Hotel Boom with Purchase of 'Haunted' Property." Real Deal Los Angeles. May 18, 2016. www.therealdeal.com.

Cornfield, Greg. "Slate Property, Atalaya Capital Joint Venture Provides $30M Loan for LA's Cecil Hotel." Commercial Observer. December 23, 2020. www.commercialobserver.com.

Deininger, Keith. "*American Horror Story* Season 5: The True Story of the Cecil Hotel." Screen Rant. March 29, 1920. www.screenrant.com.

DeVilla, Joey. "A Dump with a Future (Or: My Review of the Cecil Hotel)." *Adventures of Accordion Guy in the 21st Century*. November 3, 2008. www.joeydevilla.com.

Devine, Lucy. "The Cecil Is Currently Closed but It Plans to Open Soon." Tyla. February 12, 2021. www.tyla.com.

Dibdin, Emma. "How Downtown L.A.'s Cecil Hotel Went From Lively Destination to 'Hell on Earth.'" *Town & Country*, February 20, 2021. www.townandcountrymag.com.

Donahue, Sarah. "No Opening Date in Sight for the Cecil Hotel." LADT News. April 3, 2021. www.ladowntownnews.com.

Evans, Donna. "The Strange Saga of the Cecil Hotel." LADT News. June 26, 2014. www.ladowntownnews.com.

Fernandez, Jackie. "Decomposing Body in Water Tank, Suicide, Murder: LA Council's Pick for Hotel Historic Monument." MyNewsLA.com. February 28, 2017. www.mynewsla.com.

Firehouse. "L.A Firefighter Allegedly Lied About Stabbing." February 2, 2011. www.firehouse.com.

Fleming, Mike, Jr. "Jeremy Lovering to Helm Sony Horror 'The Bringing,' Inspired by Cecil Hotel." *Deadline*, August 21, 2014. www.deadline.com.

Fowler, Kate. "True-Crime Fan Collects Tap Water from Cecil Hotel, Sparks Criticism." *Newsweek*, July 7, 2021. www.newsweek.com.

Ghost Adventures. "Cecil Hotel." New York: Discovery Plus, January 4, 2021.

Guardian. "Is the Cecil Hotel the Most Haunted Hotel in Los Angeles." November 14, 2016. www.theguardian.com.

Guzman, Richard. "Shake-Up at Main Street Low-Income Housing Complex." LADT News. April 10, 2012. www.ladowntownnews.com.

Hamacher, Tara. "Los Angeles Department of City Planning Cultural Monument Application." December 15, 2016.

Hamilton, Denise. "A Serial Killer Who Crossed Continents." *Los Angeles Times*, November 27, 2007. www.latimes.com.

Harris, Chris. "Samuel Little, Serial Killer Who Confessed to 93 Murders, Dies at 80." Apple News. December 31, 2020. www.apple.com.

Hasenplug, Jade. "Who Murdered Elizabeth Short, the Black Dahlia?" Soapboxie. October 9, 2020. www.soapboxie.com.

Hemmerlein, Sandi. "Where to Explore Downtown L.A.'s Most Historic Hotels." KCET. November 26, 2019. www.kcet.org.

Henry, Erica, and Greg Botelho. "L.A. Hotel Sued Over Corpse Found in Water Tank." CNN. March 1, 2013. www.cnn.com.

Hodel, Steve. February 27, 2019. www.stevehodel.com.

Homicide Report. "Serial Killer: Louis Craine." *LA Times*, August 3, 2010.

Hotel Executive. "Prominent New York City–Based Developer Expands Portfolio by Acquiring First West Coast Property." May 23, 2016. www.hotelexecutive.com.

Hot Pink Sun. "Staying at the Haunted Cecil Hotel." www.youtube.com.

Howard, Bob. "Multi-Housing Capital Advisors Launches." GlobeSt.com. July 8, 2009. www.globest.com.

Invisible People. "Los Angeles Homeless Man Shares the Harsh Reality of Skid Row." August 10, 2018. www.invisiblepeople.tv.

Ishak, Natasha. "The Unsolved Mystery Behind the Disturbing Death of Elisa Lam." July 10, 2021. allthatsinteresting.com.

Khouri, Andrew. "Once a Den of Prostitution and Drugs, the Cecil Hotel in Downtown L.A. Is Set to Undergo a 100-Million Dollar Renovation." *Los Angeles Times*, June 1, 2016. www.latimes.com.

Lordan, John. *Brain Scratch*, "Lisa Lam Episode." www.youtube.com.

Malnik, Eric. "Goldie Osgood." *Los Angeles Times*, June 6, 1964. www.latimes.com.

McAuliffe, Cat. "12 Strange and Creepy Things That Happened at the Cecil Hotel." Graveyard Shift. February 28, 2020. www.ranker.com.

Meares, Hadley. "Lost Landmarks." KCET. September 29, 2015. www.kcet.org.

————. "The Suicide." KCET. September 29, 2011. www.kcet.org.

Merryweather, Cheish. "Ten Creepiest Events That Happened at the Cecil Hotel." Creepy. September 10, 2018. www.listverse.com.

Miller, Julie. "About the Time Sean Penn Exchanged Notes with a Serial Killer." *Vanity Fair*, March 10, 2015. www.vanityfair.com.

Murderpedia. "Bobby Jo Maxwell." "Johann Jack Unterweger." "Stephen Nash." "Robert Marcus Burgunder Jr." www.murderpedia.org.

Murtaugh, Taysha. "The Creepy History of Los Angeles' Cecil Hotel." Country Living. October 13, 2017. www.countryliving.com.

Nilles, Billy. "From the Black Dahlia to *American Horror Story*: Inside the History of Los Angeles' Deadliest Hotel." Asean. February 19, 2019. www.a seanow.com.

Owens, Craig. "Los Angeles Cecil Hotel Deaths." Bizarre Tales, Haunted LA. March 20, 2016. www.bizarrely.com.

PBS NewsHour. "In LA, Poverty on Skid Row Defies US 'Humane Reputation.'" October 28, 2018. www.pbs.org.

Pietra, Xavier. "Hotel of Horrors: The Dark and Terrifying History of L.A.'s Cecil Hotel." Lineup. June 4, 2019. www.the-line-up.com.

Prosper, Dr. Daniel, "Los Angeles Citywide Historic Context Statement, Hotels 1870–1980." SurveyLA. July 2017. www.HistoricPlaces.org.

Pullham, Mark. "The Vienna Strangler and the Crime Writer." *Crime Magazine*, November 1, 2010. www.crimemagazine.com.

Real Monsters. "Richard Ramirez." November 8, 2019. www.serialkillers.com.

RnK AllDay. "Once Upon a Time in Skid Row." Slumpire. September 6, 2019. missionariaprotectiva.blogspot.com.

Ryall, Jenni. "Before the Ghost Photo: The Disturbing, Gruesome Past of the Cecil Hotel." January 1, 2014. www.news.com.au.

Rylah, Juliet Bennett. "Cecil Hotel Employee Explains How He Found the Body of Elisa Lam." LAist. October 2, 2015. www.laist.com.

————. "New York Developer Reveals His Plans to Give the Cecil Hotel a Hip Makeover." LAist. May 31, 2016. www.laist.com.

Scott, Anna. "Upgrade Stirs Trouble at Cecil Hotel." LADT News. February 4, 2008. www.ladowntownnews.com.

Serena, Katie. "The Chilling Story of Murder and Hauntings Inside Los Angeles' Cecil Hotel." ATI. October 15, 2019. www.allthatsinteresting.com.

Serial Killing. Episode 191, "Richard Ramirez." Podcast. June 7, 2019. https:// Anchor.fm/app.

Siskel, John. *Biography*. "Serial Killer Files: Jack Unterweger." April 11, 2017. www. youtube.com.

Smith, Jennifer. "New Details on Elisa Lam's Mysterious Death." *Daily News*, November 28, 2019.

Steve Hodel. www.stevehodel.com.

Tripadvisor. "The Cecil Hotel." www.tripadvisor.com.

True Crime All the Time. Episodes 64 and 65, "Richard Ramirez: The Night Stalker." February 4 and 11, 2018. www.truecrimeallthetime.com

University of North Carolina. "Ed Burns." 2020. www.blackdahlia.web.unc.edu.

Warren, David. "Capturing the Vienna Woods Killer." *Vienna Review*, June 22, 2011. www.theviennareview.at.

Wattenhofer, Jeff. "Can a Hip New York Hotelier Gentrify LA's Notoriously Nightmarish Cecil Hotel?" Curbed LA. December 8, 2015. www.la.curbed.com.

Westmaas, Reuben. "The Cecil Hotel is Known as L.A.'s Most Haunted for Many Horrifying Reasons." Discovery. August 1, 2019. www.discovery.com.

Wikipedia. "Cecil Hotel." www.en.wikipedia.org.

———. "Christopher Dorner Shooting and Manhunt." www.en.wikipedia.org.

———. "Death of Elisa Lam." www.en.wikipedia.org.

———. "George Hodel." www.en.wikipedia.org.

———. "List of Deaths and Violence at the Cecil Hotel." www.en.wikipedia.org.

———. "Los Angeles in the 1920s." www.en.wikipedia.org.

———. "Skid Row, Los Angeles." www.en.wikipedia.org.

———. "Skid Row Stabber." www.en.wikipedia.org.

———. "Vaughn Greenwood." www.en.wikipedia.org.

Winterfeldt, Maggie. "OMG, the Real American Horror Story Hotel Is Scarier Than the Show." POPSUGAR. January 14, 2016. www.popsugar.com.

Yelp. "The Cecil Hotel." www.yelp.com.

ABOUT THE AUTHOR

 **D**ale Richard Perelman has also written *Mountain of Light: The Story of the Koh-I-Noor Diamond, The Regent: The Story of the Regent Diamond, Centenarians: One Hundred 100-Year-Olds Who Made a Difference, Lessons My Father Taught Me, Steel: The History of Pittsburgh's Iron and Steel Industry 1852–1902, Road to Rust: The Disintegration of the Steel Industry in Western Pennsylvania and Eastern Ohio, New Castle's Kadunce Murders* and *The Scottish Rite Cathedral* (cowritten with Rob Cummings).

Perelman is currently completing a book on former baseball player and Pittsburgh Pirates manager Chuck Tanner. Perelman holds a bachelor of arts degree in English literature from Brown University, an MBA from the Wharton School of the University of Pennsylvania, a gemologist's designation from the GIA and a summer writer's certificate of completion from Yale University.